D1563825

The Gift of Wings

an autobiography of

a life in the sky

3⁰⁰

888 776-3766

W·D—

✳ 6306457 ✳
STAR   STAR

victoria

Other Books by Ben Mukkala:

"Thoughts Along the Way - Secrets of a Happy Life" Selected Columns

"Life is Not a Destination"

Audio Version, "Life is Not a Destination"

"Touring Guide, Big Bay & Huron Mountains"

"Come On Along, Tales and Trails of the North Woods"

"Copper, Timber, Iron and Heart, Stories from Michigan's Upper Peninsula"

See page 309 for ordering information.

The Gift of Wings

an autobiography of a life in the sky

by
Ben Mukkala

Still Waters Publishing
Marquette, Michigan
© 2008

The Gift of Wings

an autobiography of
a life in the sky

Copyright © 2008
Ben Mukkala

All Rights Reserved
No part of this document may be copied or reproduced
in any way without the express permission
of the author.

All photography in this book is the work of the author
unless indicated otherwise.

Published by Still Waters Publishing, 2008

Printing Coordinated by Globe Printing, Ishpeming, Michigan
www.globeprinting.net

Limited First Edition • 2000 copies • November 2008

ISBN 978-0-9709971-7-3

*Cover photo - Major Ben Mukkala, a lieutenant at the time this
photo was taken, in a T-33 Cockpit.*
Back cover photo - Boeing B-47 "Stratocruiser"

Dedication

John Gillespie Magee, Jr. (1922-1941)

Oh! I Have slipped the surley bonds of earth
And danced the skies on laughter-silvered wings;
Sunward I've climbed, and joined the tumbling
mirth
Of sun-split clouds and done a hundred things
You have not dreamed of - wheeled and soared
and swung
High in the sunlit silence. Hov'ring there,
I've chased the shouting wind along, and flung
My eager craft through footless halls of air.
Up, up the long, delirious burning blue
I've topped the wind-swept heights with easy grace
Where never Lark, nor even Eagle flew -
And while with silent lifting mind I've trod
The high untrespassed sanctity of space,
Put out my hand and touched the face of God.

And to John and Sig and Stan and all you guys upon whose shoulders I have climbed to "dance the skies on laughter-silvered wings."

TABLE OF CONTENTS

For my children:

Now you know where your Daddy was all the time.

Love
Daddy

In the Beginning

It all pretty nearly ended with a carnival ride. There used to be an open field on the eastern shore of Teal Lake up near Negaunee in Michigan's Upper Peninsula. It was the place where all the traveling road shows used to stop and set up. I was a teenager at the time and that hurdy-gurdy music was like the pied piper. This particular carnival had all the rides and sideshows and throw-the-ball-at-the-milk-bottle games but it also had this one particular ride. I believe it was called "Tilt-a-Whirl," something like that. There was a vertical arm maybe thirty feet long with the center attached to a pivot on a vertical support. At each end of that arm it had a small cocoon-like cage with slightly padded leather seats and seat belts to hold a person in. There was room in each cocoon for two riders (barely).

I watched several people ride this thing. The arm went round and round and the cocoon rolled left and right and completely over. As I watched I thought, "Ya know that looks a lot like

John Wayne flying his P-40 Warhawk in that World War II 'Flying Tigers' movie. I'll just give 'er a try and see if this flying thing is for me."

I paid my quarter and the guy helped strap me and another fella in. Then he latched that cocoon door around us. He pulled a lever and the arm started going up and around and down and around. People were screaming and I quickly had no idea which way was up or which way was down.

The arm went up and around and the cocoon rotated first this way and then that. I lost all sense of orientation and was quickly reduced to hanging on with both hands wide eyed and some concerned – in other words I was scared! The other guy in the cocoon with me lost more than that – yuck!

I thought that ride was only supposed to last a couple minutes but it seemed to go on forever. At long last the rig stopped. The cocoon rolled upright. The guy operating the thing unlatched the cage. I managed to get the belts and straps unhooked and struggled to crawl out.

When I tried to stand up I almost fell over. The fella running the thing caught my arm. I guess he

Alone on a Wide Wide Sea

was used to reactions like that. After I had walked away and convinced my stomach it should stay where it was supposed to be I had made a decision about John Wayne and his flying. I vowed I was going to be a farmer or a ditch digger for the rest of my life. Well, it didn't quite happen that way. Let me tell you about it.

"Boot" camp

The Recruit

I was working as a "grease monkey," a wannabe mechanic in a local garage. There was no particular direction to life at the time. I had just turned 20 years old, was a couple years out of high school and was taking my fun where I found it. This was 1950. The Korean War was going strong.

The loudspeaker in the garage crackled to life and I was called to the phone. The phone call came from the sister of a friend of mine who worked at the local draft board. United States President Harry S. Truman was sending out greetings to a number of us, a call for recruits for the military via our local draft boards, "Greetings!" his announcement would say. "You have been selected etc." Some of you may remember that. Anyway, this considerate young lady had called to tell me that my draft notice had been sent out that day.

Back then, once you had received your draft

notice your butt belonged to the draft board. It was either the Army or the Marine Corp, whoever needed men at the time. Before receiving that notice a fella was free to enlist in whatever branch of the service he chose – as long as he was qualified. I thanked the lady for her consideration. I then explained my situation to the shop foreman and asked him for a little time off.

I had seen the war movies with John Wayne crawling around in the mud on some of those Pacific islands. That didn't appeal to me at all. I figured the Navy might be the place for me. They had to have water to float all those boats and a fella ought to be able to wash up now and then.

On the way to the recruiting station I stopped at a corner café and happened upon a couple friends of mine, Calvert Gentz and Milo Palm. They, too, were anticipating their draft notices. Over coffee we commiserated with each other and discussed the pros and cons of the situation. It was decided that if I would agree to join the Air Force, they would too. We could all go together.

The recruiting Sergeant seemed happy to see us and assured me that, with my experience in garages, "in a couple months you'll be overhauling aircraft engines." That sounded good to me. We all signed on the dotted line and in just a couple days we were on a railroad train to San Antonio, Texas.

The train accumulated a good number of recruits along the way. We all stumbled out of the train in Texas to line up "like four rows of corn." I was in the second row. Calvert and Milo were in the third. I went to the left. They went to the right. That was the end of the "go together" business.

Basic training was a change from the happy go lucky civilian life of a few days before. The first thing the military does is remove everything that made a person what they were. Your hair – gone! Civilian clothes – gone! Control of your own time – gone! The only acceptable answers were, "Yes, Sir!" "No, Sir!" and, "No excuse, Sir!" Always with the "Sir!" on the end. A person learns to adapt or live in misery – or both.

I remember that recruiter telling me "you'll be overhauling aircraft engines?" Ha Ha. After basic training I was sent to a radio repair school at Scott Air Force Base in Illinois. I didn't really mind as it was clean work and very interesting. I also decided I would apply for officer's candidate school and become a Second Lieutenant,

The Corporal who took my application for officers training wasn't very encouraging. When he found out I didn't have any college classes he told me I had no chance of being approved. He didn't say I couldn't apply though. He did say that, without the credit allowance given for a minimum of two years of college, he didn't know of anyone who had been accepted.

It turned out he was right. I wasn't accepted. That was a blow to my ego.

I did manage to complete the radio repair school with a high enough score that I was promoted to Corporal. That made me feel a little better.

From Illinois I was sent to Carswell Air Force Base at Fort Worth, Texas. The aircrafts there were B-36 "Peacemaker" bombers built by Consolidated Vultee Aircraft Corporation, "Convair.". They were BIG airplanes. Each aircraft had six reciprocal engines with twenty-eight cylinders each and four additional jet engines. When those ten throttles were pushed forward for maximum power on take off, the whole earth shook. This was an impressive machine.

I arrived at Carswell as a radio repairman, airborne equipment, but was immediately transferred to Electronic Counter Measures, "ECM." The equipment was electronic transmitters and receivers, just like radios, but whereas radios were intended to allow people to talk with one another, ECM was intended to keep folks from communicating with one another. This was a real cloak-and-dagger type operation and was extremely interesting stuff. That ECM experience could be a whole story in itself but I'd better stay on track.

My intention when enlisting in the Air Force had been to serve my required enlistment and go back home. Those fates that control a person's life must have had a good laugh over that. I was to be stationed at Carswell Air Force Base several times during my years in the Air Force.

Maybe some of you may remember this turn of events in the Korean War. General MacArthur had pushed the North Koreans all the way up to the Yalu River, the Korean border with China. Then the hammer fell! The Chinese Army came rolling south across the river. There were hundreds of thousands of them. When they charged, only the front ranks were armed. The Chinese charging behind that front line were empty handed. The tactic was that they should pick up the weapon of those in front as they were shot down and press on. Geeeezus! Our guys didn't have ammunition enough to shoot them all. Anyway, for the rest of us, the Air Force suddenly needed fighter pilots – BADLY. They did away with the two year college requirement. The rule now was if you could see light and hear thunder, they wanted you.

The Enlisted Life

(Note: This is a story that was included in my book "Life is Not a Destination" published in 2005. It's a favorite story of mine so I have included it again here. Maybe you've read it – maybe not. I'd rather you had a second chance than to have missed it. (Thank you for your understanding.)

I'm gonna share something with you here. It happened in the recent past but brought to mind – well – you'll see what I mean. I thought I'd plug it in here as something to make you smile, maybe reminisce yourself in your easy chair. This is "everyday life" at its happiest and best

It wasn't too long ago that I got an e-mail, you know, one of those electronic letters you get on the computer. It started out, "Are you the Ben Mukkala that was stationed down in Fort Worth back in 1952 when . . ." and it went on describing Air Force life at Fort Worth. It was signed Richard T. Nicolls, M.D.

1952! Boy! That was a long time ago. But I was there and I was the guy he was asking about. By way of telling him I was that fella I sent back a message I felt he should be able to identify with.

"If you're the guy I danced with . . ." Now before your imagination gets carried away, I'd better start that story from the beginning.

Back in 1952 three of us, young Air Force guys, Richard "Nick" Nicolls from San Bernadino, California, Donald McFadden from up around Boston, Massachusetts, and me, from Michigan, were all stationed at Carswell Air Force Base at Fort Worth, Texas. On the evening I was recalling to him we all three had dates with three lovely young ladies, friends of one another, in Fort Worth.

The evening was going nicely with drinks and dinner and drinks and dancing and drinks and, well – and Nick might argue with me here – Nick had dipped into the barrel of "Old Cordwood" maybe a little too deeply. His date had become a bit upset with his making merry. Shucks, we had all been toasting one another in a rather unrestricted fashion. Anyway his date in particular was concerned with his driving, perturbed with the way the evening was proceeding and, well, in short, she was PO'd.

We had stopped at a little watering hole with a small dance floor on the second floor. For any of you who might be familiar with Fort Worth, this was out along Camp Bowie Boulevard on the west side of town. The mood of the group had become reserved. Nick's date was downright chilly.

We had stopped, parked Nick's car, gone upstairs and found a table. We ordered drinks and settled in.

This was one of those secluded spots and on this night it wasn't overly crowded. In an attempt to lighten the atmosphere and bring a little gaiety to the proceedings – I guess that's what he had in mind – Nick rose in a most gentlemanly manner and asked his date to dance. Not a good move under the circumstances. His date raised her pretty little head, poked out her pretty little chin and replied with a distinct, frigid and definite "No!" Taken aback but not a bit discouraged Nick flamboyantly turned to my date and repeated his request. My young lady squirmed a little uncomfortably, shot a surreptitious glance at her companions, looked down at her drink and replied "No, thank you" but in a more subdued tone. Still not recognizing the futility of his mission or maybe just being bull-headed, Nick plowed on determined to "live in fame or go down in flames." He turned to Don's date and again repeated his offer. Same response. There he was, standing beside the dance floor – alone.

You guys all know what that's like. It was obvious by now to the whole establishment. He was making his pitch to these young ladies and he was striking out.

I strongly suspect that from the age of about three girls are aware that they have the capability of crushing the confidence, the self-image, the joie de vivre, the ego of any young fella. Our would-be Don Juan may boldly walk across a dance floor in a crowded bistro to ask the lady of his choice to dance. There are various ways she can refuse but that brief, sharp one syllable response, "No," can crush him to powder. For our would-be great lover it may have been a short but enjoyable stroll across the floor with his request. After that curt refusal it is a long and painful crawl back across a hostile desert. Everyone is watching – and they all know. Every step of the way he's trying to invent a plausible face-saving story to tell his friends.

This was the situation that was rapidly becoming clear to Nick's otherwise confident composure – or maybe not.

With nowhere to hide and not wanting to face that "long walk" back around the (little) table to his seat, he turned to me. "Would you care to dance?" he asked in his most eloquent manner.

"Why, certainly," I replied graciously. And we did. We danced.

That is to say we began dancing – I don't remember who was leading. Our young ladies went into shock reacting as if we had suggested that their mommas and poppas hadn't known one another very well.

Don McFadden leaned back and guffawed loudly and long startling the whole establishment.

Our sudden fame gained us some notoriety among the patrons of the place. Our actions were a little too much for management to accept. This was before the days of "Gay Rights" and "don't ask, don't tell."

The bouncer, a big burly guy who hangs out near the end of the bar in all places of this sort walked out on the dance floor. He quietly made Nick and me "an offer we couldn't refuse." He suggested that maybe we should leave.

McFadden was still laughing so hard he could

hardly walk down the stairs.

The girls, well, to say they were flustered is an understatement. I overheard a tense under-the-breath comment of one to another, "Everyone was looking at us!"

Of course Nick and I were upset too. We hadn't gotten to finish our dance.

Needless to say there was no "parking and sparking" after that little episode. Matter of fact I don't believe we ever saw those girls again. Ah, well, there were a lot of pretty girls in Fort Worth. And, what the heck, we were Air Force men - braving the wild blue yonder - keeping the world safe – "Peace was our Profession," all that sort of thing. This might have been one minor disappointment but none of us even got out of step – one for all and all for one – "and all that jazz."

Anyway that's what that message, sent to me "in the dark," lit up in my memory. There were many more memories and I'm sure Nick and I will talk them over. I imagine most of it will be on the e-mail as he's out in the state of Washington while I'm in Northern Michigan.

We both wondered about Don McFadden – I

think it was Sewickley, Massachusetts he was
from but neither of us could find him. I wonder
whether we'll ever cross paths with him again.
From what I remember of Don, he may be in jail
somewhere. If you're out there Don, give us a
holler.

Well that's a tale from the misty past.

Nick decided one day that he would apply
for pilot training. The Korean War wasn't going
that well and the Air Force had opened the door
to flying training a little wider. Nick was now
qualified. So was I.

Nick was a rather meticulous fella and had
picked up two application forms – in case he
should make an error on the first one. He talked
to me about this opportunity but I had been bit
once already back at the radio school. I didn't
want to be put down again. Dick didn't make
any mistakes on his first application and talked
me into filling out the second one. He said he
would take care of turning it in.

T-6 "Texan" Trainer

The Aviation Cadet

The next thing Nick and I knew we were both told to report to the base hospital for examinations. Some of those tests were rather strange but I guess they were checking coordination and trying to determine our psychological make up.

Nick had a bad break during the physical examination. I don't know the technical term but the problem was described like this: if he was looking to his left and shifted his eyes to the right, one eye shifted immediately but the other eye tracked over slower. That hadn't presented Nick with any problems in the past but was enough to disqualify him. And me? The guy with no college? The guy who hadn't even done that well in High School? Why I sailed right through. Evidently the war was going worse than we thought.

I was sent to a civilian contract flying school at Columbus, Mississippi, as a member of Cadet Class 53F.

The first four weeks or so at Columbus were

When a cadet got demerits during an inspection they had to be "walked off" on the tour ramp.

spent in ground school. We learned about aircraft, engines, weather, navigation and marching. We were also taught how to "eat a square meal." Upperclassmen supervised the lower class – harassed them is a better description. Part of this "pressure," I believe, was another evaluation of a person's psychological make up. They wanted to see how a person would conduct himself under pressure. During meals, we the underclass, had to sit at attention, arms at our sides, spines erect and straight, eyes fixed forward. You learned to sort of feel around your plate helped by your peripheral vision to find your food. If an upperclassman asked a question, you had three chews and a swallow and were then expected to answer with no food in your mouth. Correct posture. No elbows on the table. Small bites. I think a lot of us lost some weight while underclassmen.

Finally we were scheduled to go to the flight shack, the operations office down on the flight line, the area where the airplanes were parked. That was excitement. The training aircraft were quite famous, the North American Aircraft built T-6 (we had model "G"s) "Texan" which had already trained a multitude of military pilots. Our first few sessions on the flight line were spent learning to start the engine, check the engine instruments, taxi the aircraft or "walk the wing," stay by the wing tip while another junior aviator and his instructor taxied the aircraft. The idea was an additional safeguard against clipping another airplane with the wingtip.

Then came the day when we would actually "slip the surly bonds of earth" and fly! You pushed the throttle forward all the way. Four hundred and fifty horsepower roared to life. The airplane suddenly tried to turn left. You pushed the right rudder pedal in an attempt to correct it – and you did – too much correction and it started to go right.

Life was suddenly very exciting! With the help of the instructor you managed to get the aircraft into the air without hitting anything or "ground looping," the torque or rudder-overcorrection causing the airplane to spin around in a circle.

We were taught coordination, orientation and "how to fly." After a couple weeks, maybe three or four flights under my belt, I spoke privately to my instructor, a civilian but a former Air Force pilot named Otis Allison. I suggested that maybe this flying thing wasn't for me. I'm sure I left my fingerprints in the metal cowling of several of those aircraft, hanging on for dear life. The instructor seemed surprised and said he thought I was doing well. I told him I was scared. He said that was a good thing, that I should never lose a deep respect for a machine that had the ability to do me great harm. With his encouragement I pressed on and I'm certainly glad that I did. Thank you, Otis Allison, wherever you may be.

We managed to control the aircraft after a fashion – and at least manage not to run into one another – we flew to a sod airstrip and began working on how to land. That is really the only absolute essential in learning to fly. Nothing else has that ultimate certainty. A person can avoid taking off, not have to perform turns and stalls and the rest of the maneuvers but, as was pointed out, they have "never left an airplane up there yet."

Three supervised solo flights at the sod training field, three landings each time, and your instructor "signed you off" to fly - alone - anywhere within the local area! What a feeling that was!

That morning I was assigned an aircraft. I carefully preflighted the machine, checked the fuel, the tires and wiggled the control surfaces, acted like I really knew what I was doing. The engine start went off without a hitch. I taxied out, ran the engine up, checked the magnetos and the engine instruments and I was ready to go – alone – all by myself into the "wild blue."

A T-6 has a greenhouse type canopy, windows all around from shoulder level up. For takeoffs and landings the canopy, that part around the cockpit, would be slid back, it would be open. If there were any problems on the ground you could readily get out. With the canopy open the wind would howl around you as you took off. My canopy was open. I called the control tower and was cleared to taxi onto the runway and take off.

I pushed the throttle forward. By now I had learned to control the tendency for the plane to turn left. The tail came up into the air. We, the plane and I were going faster - and faster. I was ready to take off!

Gentle back pressure on the control stick and that roaring, vibrating, wind-whistling mass of power and aerodynamic excellence rose into the air. How sweet it is!

There seemed to be a little mist, moisture of some kind spraying on my face. Must be a little rain, I guessed. Rain? Rain? I looked up and around. The sun was shining and the sky was a beautiful blue. Where was the rain coming from? I took my hand off the throttle and wiped my face. I looked at my hand. It was covered with oil. Oil? Where was the oil - -oh my God! The engine was leaking oil!

"Mayday! Mayday! Mayday!" I shouted into the microphone. Mayday is a universal radio call to alert anyone within hearing that you are in a plenty scared, life-threatening emergency.

My immediate concern now was to get that airplane back onto the ground. If that engine ran out of oil and quit I'd be on the ground whether I chose to or not. I desperately wanted to be able to choose where the ground and I would get together.

This was the beginning of a training period at the Air Base and there were many airplanes in the air and even more on the airport taxiways awaiting clearance to take off. There was a sudden period of dead silence on the radio before the control tower came on the air.

"Aircraft calling Mayday, what is your call sign and position?" Everybody else on radios and in all the other aircraft on the ground stopped, waiting and listening.

I was floundering around in the cockpit, the airplane probably lurching up and down several hundred feet as I tried to analyze the situation further. "This is Air Force seven one eight. I just took off on runway zero nine. I blew an oil line on take off and request an immediate landing."

"What is your position, seven one eight?"

"Ah, yah, I'm turning downwind for zero nine left."

"You're cleared for an immediate landing on runway zero nine left. The wind is one zero zero degrees at six knots."

The engine was roaring along comfortably and gave no indication of any trouble. I quickly went through the pre-landing check, the "GUMP check: Gas on the fullest tank, Mixture full rich, Propeller control full increase. What did I miss? Oh yeah, the "G" for gear, landing gear. Better get the wheels down. My safety belt and shoulder harness were in the locked position.

I managed a look outside the cockpit and down at the ground. Red lights were flashing as fire trucks and the ambulance raced to the runway I was to land on.

By now I am turning on the base leg, the descending flight path just before the turn to the final approach to the runway. I looked out again. There, on the taxiway, were a dozen or more other aircraft, stopped. They were all turned slightly so the people in the front and rear cockpits could both watch me.

There was a frozen instant in time that I remember clearly and distinctly to this day. I looked at all those faces looking up at me and thought, "You bunch of bloodthirsty so-and-sos are watching to see me crash. Well, I'm going to disappoint you!"

I continued on down the final approach and made one of the sweetest landings anybody anywhere has ever seen. So there! (All pilots exaggerate a little bit, you know.)

With the wheels on the ground once more the pressure was off. Fire trucks and the ambulance were racing along right beside my aircraft. I pulled the mixture back to idle cut-off to stop the engine and turned off the runway as the airplane rolled to a stop.

A fireman was up on the wing immediately checking to see if I was all right. Another guy had gone to the engine cowl and pulled off one of the panels. "Aw, it's just a hydraulic line," he called.

JUST A HYDRAULIC LINE! JUST A HYDRAULIC LINE! I was incensed! Here I had just risked life and limb in a deed of derring-do and this guy has the effrontery to say it was "just a hydraulic line."

Two fellas from the ambulance were sort of manhandling me out of the cockpit by now. I kept trying to tell them that I was all right but they didn't pay any attention. The next thing I knew

I was in the ambulance, siren howling and lights flashing on my way to the base hospital.

"Geez, fellas, I'm OK."

No matter. To the hospital.

There was no waiting. I was immediately taken to the flight surgeon's office. The flight surgeon gave me a cursory once over and asked if I was hurt.

"No. I'm OK."

"No broken bones? Bruises?"

"No. I'm OK."

"Do you feel all right?"

"I feel fine."

"You didn't skin yourself getting out of the plane or anything?"

"Nope."

"And you feel all right?"

I was settled down quite a bit by now and thought I might know what he was looking for so I replied, "If you mean do I still remember my mother's name, yes, I do. It's Bertha."

He broke into a wide grin and, chuckling, said, "Yeah, you're all right. Get on out of here."

The guys in the ambulance graciously gave me a ride back down to the flight operation's building.

I thanked them and went inside.

You'd have thought I had two heads or something. Everybody was looking at me. I guess this was my fifteen seconds of fame that we're all supposed to have at some time during out lives.

I had been scheduled to fly so I went over to the dispatcher, an older aviator with silver hair and much experience. "Do you have another airplane?" I asked.

He turned his head, looking up at me with that so-here-you-are-again look. "Have you ever noticed that little cemetery just off the end of runway zero nine?" he asked.

That question was totally unexpected and set me back on my heels, speechless.

He said, "That's for young pilots – and old dispatchers." He grinned at me. "You're outta luck. There are no more planes available."

I walked over to my group's table and sat down. Hmmm. 'Young pilots and old dispatchers' he said. I've gotta think about that.

This was required memorization for all future Military Officers

"*The discipline which makes the soldiers of a free country reliable in battle is not to be gained by harsh or tyrannical treatment. On the contrary, such treatment is far more likely to destroy than to make an army. It is possible to impart instruction and give commands in such a manner and such a tone of voice as to inspire in the soldier no feeling, but an intense desire to obey, while the opposite manner and tone of voice cannot fail to excite strong resentment and a desire to disobey. The one mode or the other of dealing with subordinates springs from a corresponding spirit in the breast of the commander. He who feels the respect which is due to others cannot fail to inspire in them respect for himself. While he who feels, and hence manifests, disrespect towards others, especially his subordinates, cannot fail to inspire hatred against himself.*"

John M. Schofield address to the class of 1879 at West Point

Instruments

After we had soloed we would be scheduled to fly alone between dual instruction rides to get even more familiar with flying, with "life in three dimensions." The T-6 trainer was a rugged little airplane or there may have been a lot of us in that little cemetery just off the end of runway zero nine. Young pilots and old dispatchers, he had said. I'll have to remember that.

We'd go up and fly in a designated area practicing stalls and, more importantly, the recovery from stalls. We had received quite extensive ground schooling in the principles of flight, how the aircraft flew and why and when it quit flying how to get it flying again. Now we were experiencing the practical applications of what we had been taught. Spins were a son of a gun. I could do them and I did them but I never really enjoyed them. The airplane has stalled and is out of control twisting round and around and heading for the ground.

If the airplane isn't built right a spin can be a

maneuver from which a pilot can't recover. Even if the airplane is built properly, if the load isn't placed correctly inside, if the "center of gravity" is near or outside the limits, it can become uncontrollable in a spin. All in all a spin is not my idea of fun flying.

Loops and rolls and all other such maneuvers can be done precisely and exactly with the pilot in full control. They aren't necessarily something you might want to do just after a greasy meal as it can tend to churn up whatever's in your stomach. As a person gains confidence in the aircraft, in their own abilities and comes to believe that the theories they taught on the ground actually work it becomes a whole lot of fun.

But then that fun ends and it's back to work again.

There was a time when, especially if a person was flying fighter type aircraft, if a pilot couldn't see where he was going, there was no need for him to go there. Those days ended with World War II. Instrument flying came to be.

Let me bore you a little bit here with some details about you and me, about our sense of balance. A person can tell if they're standing straight up and down or leaning or turning through three main senses. You can visually see what's going on. Your muscles can sense the varying pull of gravity, the shifting of your weight one way or the other. Several fluid-filled circular canals in each of your ears are filled with fluid and have tiny hairs growing out into that fluid. Whenever you turn left or right or forward or back the fluid tends to remain stationary causing the hairs to "lean" one way or the other. These three senses give a person balance.

Flying in clouds or darkness, whenever your eyes cannot see mother earth or some other level reference you have to rely on the other senses. In an airplane, twisting and turning and banking, centrifugal forces cancel out the pull of gravity and your muscular sense. The fluid and hairs in the inner ear canal are still functioning but, like a cup of coffee, after the cup has been turned for a short time, the fluid begins to turn with the cup. The hairs remain erect as the ear canal and the fluid now turn together – and when you stop turning, the fluid tends to continue thereby lying to you, telling you, you are now turning the other way. This may have happened to you after a merry-go-round ride.

When all three senses are working together they can correct one another and all goes well. In an airplane they may all lie to you. If you're a passenger it doesn't make any difference. If you're driving the plane it's a whole 'nother thing. That's where the instruments come in.

Gyros are the heart of instrument flying as, when they are spinning, they have a quality called "rigidity in space." There's an instrument called an artificial horizon, a gyro-stabilized instrument that remains parallel to the earth regardless of what the airplane does. There are other instruments too, the airspeed (how fast you're going), the vertical speed (how fast you're going up or down), the altimeter (how high in the air you are) and, well, you get the idea.

To learn to fly "on instruments" they put us in the rear cockpit and then put a canvas tent like thing over us. We can handle the controls and see the instruments but cannot see outside the airplane. It starts out kind of spooky. Again with the background and theory from the ground school applied to the actual flying confidence comes. Just as with any other skill some folks

Part of an Aircraft Instrument Panel

are better at it than others but the theory is the same for all.

The training starts just trying to hold the airplane straight and level with no reference other than those instruments, your visual senses. The sensations from your muscles are attuned to the airplane, not the earth, and the inner ear canal, well, we talked about that. The pilot has got to learn to rely on those instruments. Know, though, that there are several instruments all working in concert so if one fails, the others will show that it has. Learning to fly on instruments was work. After an hour or so "fightin' with the gages," a person was ready for a short beer and a long nap.

Crash and Burn

The training progressed, days in ground school and on the flight line. Some of the time on the flight line, between scheduled flying, we would walk wings, walk along beside the aircraft while it was taxiing among other aircraft. If it looked like a fellow cadet was about to taxi too close to another plane we could grab the aileron, the movable control on the wing of the aircraft, and push it up and down. This would cause the control stick in the cockpit to move back and forth and get the cadet's attention. When he looked our way we could point to the approaching problem.

We didn't have to wiggle the aileron much and I suspect the task was to enhance safety of course but it also provided those of us not flying with something to keep us occupied.

Between times we would sit inside operations or, more commonly, on the grass beside the aircraft parking area. A fellow cadet, John T. "Call me Jack" Lamberty was a classmate of mine. While sitting beside the ramp he would toss rocks at birds that happened to light nearby. I asked him why he was harassing the birds. "Because they can fly better than I can," he replied. It gives you an idea of how exciting life was between flights.

Evenings, after the tactical officers had gone home to their families, the upper class used to take it upon themselves to "continue our training." I mentioned that there was an old cemetery off the end of runway zero nine.

By the way, that runway description, "zero nine," was standard terminology at all airfields to identify runways. The description came from dropping the last digit of the runway's compass heading. Runway zero nine, for example, was that runway whose compass heading was zero-nine-zero degrees.

Back to the cemetery. As I mentioned earlier it was the war in Korea that generated the urgent call for more pilots, particularly fighter pilots. A fighter pilot's gotta be aggressive. The war cry among the ranks of aviation cadets was, "Every man a Tiger!"

I don't know who it was that evidently desecrated someone's grave but the upper class had somehow procured a tombstone. They attached several ropes to that big heavy stone. Evenings, after the tactical officers had gone, we underclassmen had to pull those ropes and drag that stone around the squadron area while we howled and growled and shouted, "Every man a Tiger!"

An upperclassman was god and the only answers an underclassman was permitted were, "Yes, Sir!" "No, Sir!" and "No excuse, Sir!" Period. Everyplace an underclassman went was at double-time, running.

If we didn't answer an upperclassman's questions correctly, if our "gig line" wasn't straight (that's the line from your shirt buttons through your belt buckle and the fly of your pants) or for darn near any other reason you got a "gig." Gigs had to be walked off in full "class A" uniform on weekends on the parade ground. The assigned tactical officer would inspect every now and again, the troops in formation or the barracks, and gigs would be given for any infractions. It was training but it was also harassing, a testing of your ability to handle pressure.

One of our tactical officers was a young

lieutenant who several of us believed still had a bit to learn, Anyway he was a bit carried away with himself and a little drunk with the power being a tactical officer gave him. A good number of us had come to cadets from the enlisted ranks. We weren't raw recruits. The Lieutenant had assembled all of us in a small auditorium one day to dress us down for "sloppy behavior and appearance and lack of military bearing." At the conclusion of his speech he added, "I know you cadets don't like me but I have a wife and little boy who do." From the rear ranks in a somewhat muffled voice was heard, "Wait'll the kid grows up." We all did a bit of walking off gigs that weekend.

Open ranks inspections were conducted at least weekly to be sure uniforms were neatly starched and pressed. Our barracks was also subject to inspection at any time. Foot lockers, closets and tightly made "bounce a quarter off the bunk" beds were the standards. One of the guys tried sleeping on the floor to keep his bed taut but it wasn't worth the discomfort. We washed our shorts and socks every night, hung them on a chair or whatever to dry, and put 'em on again in the morning. We were only permitted to have one pair of shorts, one T-shirt, one handkerchief and one pair of socks in our laundry bags at any time. Lemme tell you it would take a brave man to open my laundry bag. When I shipped out I just threw it way.

After six weeks or so we reached upper class status and life got considerably easier. They even gave us "Open Post," a weekend to go off base to town. The intensity and pressure of the condensed flying training was one thing but it was that time off base that did me in.

One of the fellas had a car. A bunch of us crammed in and we headed for the bright lights – well – at least for the street lights of the neighboring Mississippi towns. I managed to meet a very attractive young southern lady. She had been the queen of the annual Memphis Cotton Carnival. And I, well I was a bold and brave Aviation Cadet.

For whatever reasons you might care to imagine I am not going to delve into this adventure in any detail. Suffice it to say that the relationship resulted in my being relieved of my assignment as an aviation cadet but was recommended to attend Officers Candidate School. I reverted to my previous rank of Staff Sergeant and was transferred back to Carswell Air Force Base in Texas. The last I knew the Cotton Queen was back in Mississippi. Wherever she is, I wish her only good things and a happy life. I doubt we shall ever forget one another. The flying expression for a demise such as mine: "He Crashed and Burned." Enough said!

Never Say Die

Back at Carswell I was again assigned to ECM, the Electronic Counter Measures section. I arrived in time to join in the celebration of a birthday. Another of the troops assigned to ECM was a really nice young fella but had evidently been raised in a pretty sheltered environment. Another guy was a rather happy go lucky party-at-the-drop-of-the-hat fella whose morals, well, 'nough said. Our party guy had arranged the celebration to be held at a local dim-lit bistro that had a reputation as a good time establishment.

The party was going smashingly well and we were managing to corrupt our young airman's view of life considerably. He was, in fact, about half in the bag. Then the following occurred: Our party guy, I'll call him Al, had really outdone himself. Our young airman, I'll call him Robert, was sitting in a semi-inebriated state at a table with Al. A waitress that Al evidently knew quite well had just brought them a fresh drink. This waitress was a very foxy lady and knew how to show her equipment to its best advantage. She was wearing a tight short skirt, an extremely low cut blouse and, well, you get the picture.

The waitress leaned across the next table for whatever reason. Good-time Al took this opportunity to lightly run his hand over that even tighter tight skirt. The waitress squealed and immediately snapped erect. Al had wisely moved off. She spun around and the only person in sight was our kind and gentle half-in-the-bag young airman. He looked up with a bland smile on his face.

World heavyweight champion Joe Louis would have been proud of that waitress. There were no preliminaries. She hauled off and belted our innocent young airman knocking him clean off the chair. He wasn't physically damaged but he was shocked and confused. He groggily climbed back onto his chair. The waitress had left in a huff.

I don't think that young airman ever took another drink – for the rest of his life. He never talked much about that encounter – maybe he never even remembered it. He must have had a vague recollection that whatever had happened to him must have been someone or something bigger than himself telling him he was headed down the wrong road.

That recommendation I had received for Officers Candidate School when I left the Cadet Corps had created some disagreement back at Columbus. I had been told it had been approved - and then that it had been disapproved. The personnel officer, a young lieutenant who didn't seem to know much about the whole thing, left me with the impression that the disapproval had been approved. It was all kind of confusing. It seemed that I was out of luck. Well, never say die!

I got on the phone to Air Training Command Headquarters to find out what I could do to appeal the decision. I got 'hold of a sergeant down there. He looked up the paper work. He then told me that they were sitting on a recommendation for me to go to Officer's Candidate Training School and why hadn't I yet applied? Hooray! I was back on track!

In case you're unaware, it's the sergeants that run the services. If you want to know what's happening, don't ask the Colonel, ask the Sergeant.

I once applied for explosives demolition school. The bait was another hundred dollars a month on the paycheck. The Squadron First Sergeant called me in, poured me a cup of coffee and put his arm around my shoulder. "Son," he said – ah but that's another story for another time. I didn't go to Explosives Demolition School.

Lemme throw another story at you here. In the ECM business we had to load and unload electronic transmitters, receivers, antennas and the associated wiring onto various B-36 aircraft. This involved hauling that equipment – some of it weighing forty or fifty pounds - all over the eighty acres or so of concrete ramp on which the aircraft were parked. The wing commander had an air conditioned staff car. We had a six-by-ten-foot flat-bed four-wheel wagon. The power was all of us pulling on the wagon tongue.

The flight ramp at Fort Worth, Texas, could be a pretty hot place in the summer. I remember a picture of one of the guys frying an egg on the wing of one of the aircraft. He just cracked the egg onto the metal of the aircraft wing and it sizzled and popped.

It was also hot work hauling that wagon load of electronics around. Now and then the aircraft engine people would have to run up engines to "check 'em out." A B-36 has six 28 cylinder propeller engines. It also has a wingspan of 236 feet. They would have to pull the aircraft from its wing tip to wing tip parking space and position it parallel to the row's other aircraft. When we saw that happening we would hurry to get our wagon behind that airplane. When they started those engines we'd all climb aboard our wagon. One man would handle the wagon tongue for steering. The rest of us would unbutton our blouses and hold them out like sails. We had some pretty wild trips on that old wagon. The powers that be decided it was too dangerous to be doing that. Strange thing but they didn't say we might get hurt. They were afraid we might run into another aircraft.

As soon as I could I hustled over to the personnel office and submitted an application for Officer's Candidate School. I didn't have two years of college. Never mind. Send it in anyway. It came back approved! I had been accepted!

Stick with the Sergeants to get things done.

I was on my way to OCS at Lackland Air Force Base, San Antonio, Texas.

O C S and Beyond

Once more into the breech, dear friends. Once more an underclassman. Once more "Yes. Sir!" "No, Sir!" "No Excuse, Sir!" Once more eating square-meals. I must have been getting pretty good at it by this time.

The classes in OCS were more of a general nature concerning leadership and administration and Air Force Operation. I don't remember all the specifics but we also managed keep the surrounding area clean and trimmed and manicured to perfection.

My classmates in OCS, Class 54A, were by and large a good bunch. Oh there were a few that set you to wondering why the Lord made more of one end of the horse than he did the other but that's the way life is. I guess the contrast they created just made a person appreciate the others that much more.

We did a whole lot of marching and I volunteered to be a member of the band. I was to be a drummer. There are specialists in the art of drumming but I wasn't one of them. The attraction was that this additional duty was supposed to get a person an extra day off. Yeah! "Tell it to the Marines." We were all kept so busy we never did see any extra time off and very little time off at all. I did learn this though: when a group is marching to a band, listen to the big bass drum. The beat goes BOOM boom BOOM boom BOOM. Just remember, your left foot should be hitting the pavement with that heavy BOOM. That keeps everyone in step.

Graduation was a happy time. Many of the guys were married and wives and children attended the ceremony. As we received our commission as Second Lieutenants we all threw our hats up in the air.

I didn't anticipate any family attending as they were in Marquette, Michigan, clear across the country from San Antonio. A Sergeant I had worked for at Carswell Air Force Base had been transferred to the San Antonio area and graciously attended with his family. As it turned out my folks came down too. They had to float a loan at a local bank to afford the trip but they wanted to be there – especially my mother.

Let me tell some of you that may be reading this: Appreciate your mothers – fathers too, for that matter. By the time most of us are wise enough to realize that, we're probably a whole lot older. Unfortunately by that time the parents may no longer be around for you to show that appreciation. If you don't remember anything else in this book, remember that.

Another custom that dates back I don't know how far is that a newly commissioned officer gives a dollar to the first enlisted man to salute him. At scheduled graduation classes the troops would be waiting outside the auditorium like vultures to salute and scarf up that buck. I don't mean that in a derogatory sense. What the heck, a buck is a buck. The day I was commissioned I must have given away twenty dollars or more, a dollar at a time. I even stopped at the gate to the base, got out of the car and gave a dollar to the Air Policeman who saluted me as I was driving through. He was quite surprised but he took the dollar.

We all got a week or two off before having to report to our next duty station. With my folks, my mother, father, sister Sandra and my Aunt Jean, we were able to tour a little bit of Texas before they had to return home.

After the welcome vacation I proceeded to my next assignment. I was to return to pilot training. Oh happy day!

T-6 "Texan" in flight

Hondo by the Sea

The flight training station I was sent to this time was Hondo Air Base, about sixty miles west of San Antonio. Some of you more familiar with geography may be saying, "Sixty miles west of San Antonio? 'by the sea?'" You're absolutely correct. There's no sea anywhere near Hondo, Texas. As a matter of fact there's darn little water of any kind within miles of the place. That title, "Hondo by the Sea," was some sadistic individual's attempt at humor.

Hondo Air Base, it was said, had been a flying training base back in the 1940s, during World War II. The base was closed, abandoned after the war and leased by someone who used the barracks to raise chickens. They had cleaned the barracks up again when they re-activated the base of course but on a damp day or just after a rain there was the sense of the previous occupants "in the air." It wasn't really that bad but you definitely knew you weren't the first to tuck your head under your wing there.

Because I had had previous flying training the base operations officer decided to give me a flight check to see how much I still remembered. He took me up a couple times in the old familiar T-6 training plane and I at least managed not to crash. The result of these flights got me moved ahead a couple classes. I had no particular feelings one way or the other but when placed in this upper class, I was the new guy. I never did feel that I could put my full weight down if you know what I mean.

There was another problem of my own making. I had been a product of the "Every Man a Tiger" program and was gung ho for fighter aircraft. The commander of the flight instructors of this new group had been a bomber pilot and was admired and respected by everyone. It wasn't that I disliked him it was just that I don't seem inclined to keep my mouth shut. I managed to offend one of my fellow cadet officers to the point that he invited me to step out behind the barn, so to speak. After training one day a group of us went over to the base gymnasium and the fellow and I donned boxing gloves.

Once we were ready I turned to the guy who was to be the referee instead of paying attention to my adversary. That might not have made much difference anyway as he was a lot more into the spirit of the contest than I was. That guy was all over me like a blanket and knocked me flat on my backside. Fortunately the referee, maybe out of pity, lifted one eyelid like he knew what he was doing. I doubt he knew any more about what he was pretending to do than the man in the moon but he called the fight over and declared the other fella the winner.

I've got no excuses. I had acted like one of those half of the horses I referred to earlier and this young fella set me straight. It didn't happen right away but that guy and I later became friends. It wasn't that we'd die for one another but we were friends. Come to think of it, as I went further in the military pilot relationship, there were situations where we put our lives on the line for one another – even when you didn't know who the "other" was. Maybe I can get to one of those situations a little later in the story.

Because I had been moved forward in the training schedule, I didn't have a set number of hours to fly. The decision was that I would progress "on proficiency." This was another civilian contract school. The company was paid by the number of hours the trainees flew. There was no limit to the number of hours they could fly me. I didn't object. I got to do a whooole lot of flying.

Extra curricular activities were rather limited in the little town of Hondo. San Antonio was a short sixty miles or so down the road and many of us single troops would frequent the happy places there. There was another place a few miles north of Hondo, a place called Bandera. Bandera was a dude ranch area with a lot of partying and good times going on. Back home in Upper Michigan, the expression was "kick off the gold-seals (boots) and do the big apple." I don't know what the dude ranches called it but, being Texas, it probably had something to do with spurs. Other than the memory of chickens now and then, Hondo was a fun place.

We were approaching graduation from our primary flying school. Flying as much as I did I got to looking for new things to do while sailing around in the wild blue. I met another fella up there behind a cloud one day and we commenced a "dog fight" high in the skies over Texas. I got behind him – in his "six o'clock" position – and he couldn't shake me. He rolled over and dove into a cloud with me right on his tail. When I broke out of the cloud I didn't immediately see him. Then I picked him up below me and just off to the left. I was on him like a tiger on raw meat. He wasn't moving as fast as I was though and I shot by him about fifty feet away. When I looked over, there was someone in the rear seat. That wasn't my dog-fight buddy. That was another student – with an instructor. Big trouble!

It wasn't long after I landed that the flight

commander sent for me. He asked me what I had been doing. I said I had been flying. The interrogation went on and went nowhere. It wasn't that I was cagey or all that smart, I was just scared and for whatever reason was not admitting to anything. My flying ended, except for routine check rides and dual instruction. An investigating officer was appointed to look into the situation.

The investigating officer was a Major. I immediately got the impression that he was not going to be lenient. I was confined to my quarters – that constitutes arrest and confinement for a military officer. The investigating officer questioned the instructor who had seen me, his student and I don't know who all else. There was much "swearing in" and statements taken. I didn't get to talk to anybody.

When he asked me to write out a statement about what I had done that day, I asked him what I had been charged with? He looked at me very sternly and replied, "You know what you've done."

While all this was going on my classmates were getting orders to advanced flight training schools and were leaving the base - including the guy I had been dog-fighting with. He was sweating out his own exposure but he never came up in the investigation.

While I had been confined to the base, the flight line and my barracks, probably as much to pass the time as anything else, I got myself a copy of the "Code of Military Justice" and began to research what was happening to me and what I might expect – or not.

The Gift of Wings

And the Verdict is . . .

Eventually I received a summons, a request, whatever you want to call it to report to the base commander, a Lieutenant Colonel. I had been reading that Uniform Code of Military Justice, made a few notes and was ready to contest my treatment and whatever the charges there were as best I could.

The morning I reported, class A uniform, shoes shined and backbone ramrod straight. The operations officer, the Major who had given me my initial flight check was there too. I clicked my heels, saluted and said, "Reporting as ordered, sir."

The two of them looked at one another then back at me. The Colonel held up a paper and said, "This statement you gave the investigating officer doesn't say much at all."

"Sir, the investigating officer never did tell me what I had been charged with."

"You didn't say much about it either?"

"Sir, I have been confined to my barracks for

the last two and a half weeks. I believe that's 'arrest' and I should have been charged with something. The investigating officer never told me what I was charged with. The manual says I have the right to confront my accusers, to talk to them. I was never given that right either. Sir, I'd like to talk to a legal officer."

There was silence for a little bit as the two of them just looked at me. "We don't have a legal officer on the base."

"Then I'd like to be able to go to San Antonio, sir, to Lackland, where there is a legal officer"

Again there was a period of silence.

"You go back to your barracks. Come by again in the morning."

Well, I'd fired my best shots. I wasn't sure what was going to happen in the morning but my mind was made up. I wanted to "lawyer up," as the cop-shows are fond of saying.

The next morning, shaved, shined, showered, shampooed and in a fresh class "A" uniform I was again standing at attention before the Colonel's desk. The operations officer was there again too.

They let me stand there at attention for several

seconds – then the Colonel picked up a paper and held it out to me. "Here are your orders for advanced single-engine jet training at Bryan Air Force Base."

There was a shocked silence on my part until I finally had the presence of mind to reach out and accept the orders. The Colonel and the Major stood up. They both grinned at me and each one held out his hand.

The operations officer, the Major, as he shook my hand grinned and said, "For God's sake, Lieutenant, take it easy up there."

I managed to remember another salute before an about face and forward march. I left that office walking six feet in the air and without a parachute.

I have often wondered if that investigating officer was as unfamiliar with the Uniform Code of Military Justice as my research seemed to indicate. It seemed that my "rights" had been violated in several fundamental and basic ways. The investigation was front-page stuff all over the base. I'm sure the whole cadet corps was impressed with the swiftness and severity with which my infraction was being handled.

When the base commander and the operations officer turned me loose, I was off the base and gone before the sun went down. I imagine the fame and reputation lived long after I was gone. Maybe they were all ahead of me on this one. They had made the proper impressions on the proper troops – a sort of training exercise even though I now confess it was my wrongdoing that initiated it.

Memory Lane

I swung through San Antonio for a couple days to celebrate. Just for fun I stopped at Lackland Air Force Base and looked up the old barracks where I had been assigned my first few days in the Air Force – a recruit – a Buck Private. (It wasn't for a couple months after my enlistment before they started calling us "Airmen.")

It was still being used as a basic recruit training barracks. I parked my car beside the barracks and sort of slipped in the back door, right near where my bunk had been. There were recruits in the barracks, hair cut down to near nothing, everything hung and folded and swept. They weren't used to a Lieutenant walking in on them all alone and in the middle of the afternoon.

A couple of them leaped to their feet and would have hollered "attention" but I gave them the be-quiet sign with my hands. They just stood and stared not sure what they should do next.

I pointed to what had been my bunk those many years ago and asked, "Whose bunk is that?"

One kid, scared I had found something wrong, said a little uncertainly, "That's my bunk, sir."

"That was my bunk back in August of 1950."

By now they were relaxing a bit. I asked a couple of them where they were from. That's always a good ice-breaker. "How do you like the Air Force?" Uncertain glances again, shrugging of the shoulders. I grinned and said, "Hang in there. It gets better."

"You know, one time one of the troops had fallen asleep before lights out." The guys had gathered around to listen to my story. "We got about six guys, picked up his whole bunk and carried him out back, out onto the dry fire range. He never did wake up until the next morning when the rest of us were in formation and marching off to breakfast."

That brought a chuckle all around. About then the drill sergeant walked in to the other end of the barracks. He knew right away something was wrong. Whenever anyone, Corporal or above, enters the barracks the troops are supposed to jump to their feet and call "attention." With me in the barracks the troops came to their feet but no one called attention. I went along with it by getting to my feet, standing at attention too.

When the sergeant saw me he was somewhat surprised. I grinned at him and explained that I was just revisiting my old haunts and passing on a few "war stories." I asked about my old drill instructor and found out he was still there, a Technical Sergeant and working at Wing Headquarters. I asked him to pass on my regards, said good-by to the troops and got on out of there.

As I was driving away I caught sight of a familiar face standing beside the road. I stopped and backed up. Yes! It was Bill Hacket, an old classmate of mine from back home. We had graduated from High School together. I called out to him, "Hey, Bill! You and your buddies hop in and I'll give you a ride to wherever you're going. He had two other troops with him. They were marching to - somewhere.

Bill called "Halt" to his little detail of men and looked nervously up and down the street. It turned out he was a brand new Aviation Cadet, a recruit of sorts, and didn't think he was supposed to be taking rides. Shucks, I was a Lieutenant, wasn't I? Rank does have its privileges. "Get in the car, recruit."

I can't remember where I took them anymore and maybe Bill doesn't remember anymore either. I don't think anyone saw him so he probably didn't get in any trouble. If he did have a problem he could always blame it on the lieutenant.

I guess it was time I moved on before I screwed up the whole training command.

J-33 Jet Trainer "Shooting Star

Single Engine Jets

Bryan Air Force Base was another step along the road. I gained some fame when I first checked in. I deposited my money in a local bank, got a checking account and signed in at the base. After settling into the barracks I walked over to the Officer's Club "for a cool one" and to get something to eat. I wrote out a check at the bar.

A day or two later I was called in to explain why I had passed a bad check at the Officer's Club. A bad check will get you known all up and down the chain of command immediately. A severe reprimand is the least you can expect. It seems I had put money in one local bank and then written a check on another bank. I'll never do that again.

The officer's quarters at Bryan were actually small apartments with a sitting room and two bedrooms. My roommate was an Irishman from Chicago, Tom O'Shaugnessy. He was a good ole boy and didn't seem to be a whole lot smarter than I was.

We had only been there a few days when we were returning to the barracks from dinner. It was raining – light but rain no less. Suddenly we could hear a mewing sound, a soft whining. "Do you hear that?"

"Yeah."

"What is it?"

We began looking around, trying to locate the source of the mewing. There it was! A kitten was sitting in the rain, poised on the edge of a barracks roof about six or eight feet in the air. It seemed it wanted to get down but either didn't know how or was afraid of the height.

Tommy said, "Aw, the poor kitty."

I said, "Tom, leave the cat alone. Its momma will find it."

"But it's getting all wet."

"Tommy, leave it alone."

You should never try to argue with an Irishman who has has a couple of drinks.

"Ben, we gotta help that poor kitten. Here! Help me reach up there."

We recovered the kitten and Tommy cuddled and talked to it as we continued back to the barracks.

Tommy picked up an extra half pint of milk at breakfast, stole a small bowl and brought it back to our apartment. He set out the milk in the bowl and the kitten greedily ate its breakfast. Tom and I had to go to ground school and the flight line. We didn't get back to the barracks until later that evening.

The kitten had made itself at home and, when we returned, it was curled up on my bunk napping. The milk bowl was empty. Guess where it had chosen to, aah, "take a crap?"

T-28 "Trojan" aircraft

Tommy picked up the kitten, not nearly as caringly as the night before, and it was out the door never to return.

Flight Training at Bryan Air Force Base began in the 800 horsepower single engine propeller driven T-28 "Trojan" aircraft. It was bigger than the old T-6 and a lot more comfortable too. It had a tricycle landing gear rather than the conventional "tail dragger" three point T-6 landing gear. It was a whole lot easier to control on the ground. The cockpit was roomier and the pilot sat up higher.

I enjoyed flying that airplane. Shucks, truth be told, I enjoyed flying any airplane.

We spent a short time training in the T-28 before we were introduced to the T-33 "Shooting Star" single-engine jet trainer. It was quiet. There was no torque or "P" factor effect (propeller effect) as with a reciprocating engine. It weighed about 15,000 pounds, half of that was fuel, with a jet engine that generated about 5,000 pounds of thrust. It would really go – about 500 MPH! The expression was that it would "climb like a homesick angel." I guess that's said by pilots of many aircraft but it was appropriate for us at this stage of our training.

We were introduced to formation flying, a lead aircraft and one or more aircraft flying beside it. There's a saying, and it is true as far as I'm concerned, that "any fool can fly on the wing but it takes a good pilot to lead." If the leader is smooth and precise it's so much easier to hold a position on his wing. It can be stressful trying to maintain a precise position and can lead, among other things, to hyperventilation.

Hyperventilation occurs when your breaths are short and rapid and your muscles are tense.

This can also bring on a loss of consciousness. One of the guys, flying solo in a formation, was seen to drift out of formation and dive right into the ground. Hyperventilation and a loss of consciousness was the only explanation the accident investigation could come up with.

One of the fellas burst into the barracks one evening with great news! He had been down to Houston and had met some models down there. Good lookin' ladies! Were we interested? Was the Pope Catholic? You bet your boots we were.

It was all set up for the following night. We'd be cutting our schedules pretty close and would have to "sleep fast" if we got back in time to sleep at all but the testosterone was up and we were eager. These were models! Does it get any better than this?

We went to Houston in several cars, of course, and picked the ladies up. We headed for a place called "Hernando's Hideaway." No joke. That was the name of the place. It was dim lit and out of the way, as you might suspect, but we were riding high.

After just a couple of hours of drinking diet

cokes and other light drinks and not many of those, picking delicately and selectively at their food, the girls began talking about the need to go home. Go home? The evening was just beginning and they wanted to go home? Well, they apologized profusely. It wasn't because they weren't having a good time but they had an "early shoot" in the morning and they had to get a full night's sleep. They didn't eat much because they had to watch their figure. They limited their drinks to soft, nonalcoholic diet types because they didn't dare to look "washed out" the next day. There was nothing for it but to take them home. It had been a blow-out, a disappointing evening – up to here.

Somebody suggested we go down to Post Office Street in Galveston, just down the road. For those of you not familiar with that area in the mid 1950s, it was a place where the good times rolled. Our primary target had been a washout but our overall mission turned out to be quite a success.

Former interceptor pilot Jack Lamberty
Beside F-86 D Interceptor
Wright Patterson AFB Air Museum

Onward and Upward

Graduation from training at Bryan Air Force Base had us all awaiting the orders that would determine our Air Force future. Rumors and speculation spread through the ranks in an attempt to forecast where and to what advanced aircraft each of us might be assigned.

I am convinced that throughout the training program each of us was graded, not only on our flying skills but equally on our attitudes and character. Overriding all, of course, was what the service needed at the time. It was the need for fighter pilots as the Korean War grew more tense that had allowed many of us to qualify. Within the framework of the service' need it was pretty much accepted that fighter aircraft assignments would probably go primarily to those among us who seemed more confident and aggressive. I don't doubt there are arguments for the selection of bomber and transport pilots that can be made just as ardently. After all the speculation we waited anxiously for our assignments.

When the orders were handed out we were scattered to the four winds, so to speak. Some were more enthusiastic over their assignments than others but there wasn't anyone I remember who was really depressed.

I had been assigned to the F-86D Interceptor school at Perrin Air Force Base, just north of Dallas Texas. The cold war was on during this time and the United States had radar sites ringing the Arctic to keep watch 'lest the Russian Bear sneak bombers over the North Pole and catch us unaware. The boys in the interceptors would be defending the skies and keeping the world free for democracy.

This was before the days of electronic and/or heat-seeking air-to-air missiles. The interceptor carried "Mighty Mouse" free-flying rockets, 2 ¾" in diameter and five feet or so long. The F-86D carried a pod of 24 of these rockets and an on-board radar system to direct the fighter to the optimum firing position.

Ground radar would direct the interceptor to the area of the incoming bomber, position him on an intercepting course and the airborne radar would then compute relative speeds, allow for the predicted trajectory of the rockets and give the pilot steering information to reach that spot. Once all was aligned he was given a firing signal.

For those of you who have hunted birds with a shotgun, you probably have a clearer understanding of what we were doing: Aim the gun just ahead and above the flying bird and send off a blast of pellets (in our case, rockets) and hope that one or more would connect.

The first six weeks or so of the interceptor school was an advanced course in instrument flying. There were two weeks of ground school and an additional four weeks of flight training. The interceptor pilot, after all, would be expected to defend the skies regardless of the weather conditions.

Perrin Air Force Base was located between Sherman and Denison Texas on the Red River, the border between Texas and Oklahoma. And I was quick to note it was just a few miles from Dallas and my old stamping ground, Fort Worth. Oh happy day!

Not so happy day for the first few weeks anyway. They kept us pretty busy and Fort Worth and Dallas were sixty or seventy miles away. There were new methods of navigation being developed all the time and the basics of instrument flying to which we had been exposed were now honed and polished.

My instrument training was in the familiar T-33 and seemed to go well. I was enjoying flying even though the combination of hot Texas sun and hard work flying instruments with that tent-like hood over the cockpit was trying. I think I lost weight

There were various instrument training maneuvers we practiced, most with no practical application of their own but they were intended to polish our abilities. In the F-86 Interceptor there was only one pilot, you. In addition to controlling the aircraft you would also be expected to monitor the aircraft systems, operate the on-board radar, follow directions from a ground radar controller and defend the skies from whomever. Flying by instruments had to be second nature.

The guys who were already in the F-86 phase of training were working flying intercepts. They had to have someone to intercept. Those of us in the instrument phase would also be scheduled to fly solo, alone in the T-33s to provide targets for the students in F-86s.

We would take off, contact our local ground radar site and follow their directions. They would assign us an altitude, vector us, give us headings to fly, and direct the F-86 pilot to intercept us. I enjoyed the flying. Shucks I enjoyed any flying but I have to admit it got a little boring now and again. There were a few stunts we (there were others who got bored too) came up with to pass the time.

The T-33 carried more fuel than the F-86. We would often fly two or three hours as a target for three of four separate F-86 missions. If, for whatever reason, one of the F-86 flights didn't take off we would be directed to fly back and forth as we waited for the next mission. Radar would call us. We would answer. They would give us a turn to reverse course. We would then fly five or ten minutes on the new heading. Radar would call us again and over and over.

Radar called me. I lowered the nose of the aircraft to pick up speed. I answered. Radar called to give me the turn to reverse course. I pulled the stick back and flew into a half loop then rolled out – a maneuver called an Immelman turn, named for the World War I German fighter pilot who originated it.

The radar operator on the ground, accustomed to seeing us make a race track type turn now watched as I appeared to slow down, stop, and reverse direction. That only surprised them two or three times before they figured out what we were doing. Aah, well, it passed the time.

Something else we'd try to do. We always flew straight and level, as a bomber would be expected to do, while the interceptor was vectored in on us. We could all hear each other as we were all on the same radio frequency. The interceptor would be vectored in from a position ninety degrees from our heading – off our wing tip. The pilot had an on-board radar display, a circle with an indicator of how fast he was closing on us and a "pipper," a dot on the screen that directed him on the intercept. His job was to keep the pipper in the center of the circle.

At a position twenty seconds from what would have been his firing point his steering circle would begin to collapse. He would call out "Twenty seconds!" At this point the interceptor pilot would be totally absorbed and intent on his instruments and his radar. We in the target aircraft would often choose this call as a signal to roll our aircraft upside down and continue flying.

When the interceptor system reached the would-be firing position, the steering circle would have closed to nothing and an "X" would flash on his radar screen. He would call "Splash," and usually look up to see how he had done. He would be pretty close if all had worked out. The next decision he had to make was, is the target aircraft upside down? Or was he? Yeah, well, it was something to do.

The Gift of Wings

A change of Plans

I don't know who was making the decisions, but my schedule for F-86 interceptor training abruptly changed. I had been selected to be an instrument flight instructor. I was removed from student status and assigned as "permanent party" at Perrin Air Force Base.

They sent me to an instructor training course at Randolph Air Force Base in San Antonio. After a couple weeks there I returned to Perrin as an instructor. It took a little adjusting but I made the transition from student to instructor. I don't think there are many instructors in any subject who won't admit that a person doesn't really know anything until they try to teach it. To that I can only add, "Amen!"

Life went on. I was enjoying the flying and thoughts of burning up the highway to Dallas and/or Fort Worth kind of faded away. Hey, there were a lot of pretty girls and things to do in the Denison-Sherman area.

A few of us did manage a trip or two to Dallas

and the livin' was good. Jet aircraft were still a pretty new thing. Hollywood was grinding out jet aircraft movies, John Wayne in "Jet Pilot," things like that. With all that promotion, at parties a young lady would invariably ask, "Do you fly the jets?" We would (figuratively, of course) modestly throw our white silk scarves over our shoulder and reply, "Why, yes, I fly the jets." Do I really have to tell you where the evening went from there?

Another side trip I managed was down to Carswell Air Force Base in Fort Worth. I drove down on a Saturday and wasn't sure if any of my old buddies would be around where I could find them, I got onto the base and to the old squadron barracks area and parked the car.

Walking down the street I spied my old friend Dick "Nick" Nicolls washing his car in his fatigue uniform. I happened to be dressed in a uniform also. As I approached Nick noticed me coming but hadn't recognized me. What he saw a lieutenant approaching. He bent down and got very bust scrubbing a wheel on his car. If he didn't noticed the officer about to pass he could avoid having to come to attention and give a proper military salute. I was onto that old trick though.

When I was just behind him I stopped. Noticing "that lieutenant" had stopped, he knew the jig was up. He would have to come to attention and deliver a salute. He rose from his task, a pained expression on his face, and turned toward me.

I was already standing at attention and saluting. Nick had his hand about half way up to his forehead when he recognized me. He stopped dead in his tracks! "You son of a . .. .!" What followed was not at all proper military protocol. This was two old friends laughing and embracing each other.

I guess we finished washing the car, I don't recall. We did spend some time bringing each other up to date on what had been happening in our lives. Nick was no longer in ground maintenance but had become an aircrew member operating the radar controlled tail guns on a B-36.

We also went out "on the town" that night and celebrated. Nick is the kind of guy you wish there were more of.

The Gift of Wings

Needle, Ball and Airspeed

After I had been instructing a while a student came in who had been a World War II fighter pilot. I don't recall what all he had been doing along the way but he had risen in rank to Major. Now he really wanted to get back into the flying business. His "old days" in fighter aircraft dated back to World War II. That had been more seat-of-the-pants flying relying on seeing where he was going and what or who he was after. The instruments to which I was introducing him hadn't even been invented back then. He was having trouble. He wasn't as smooth on the stick transitioning to instrument flying as we like to see. You had to give him credit though, he was working hard.

Picture yourself in your car. The windows are all covered. The speedometer tells you how fast you're going. Another instrument, a vertical needle, will lean either left or right to tell you you're turning. A compass rose tells you in what direction you're going and your radio, by signaling a Morse code "N," a dash and a dot, or an "A," a dot and a dash, lets you know if you are left or right of the road. A steady solid tone tells you you're "on course." That's not precise but you get the idea.

We had flown a training sortie this day and wound up landing at El Paso, Texas. We climbed out of the airplane and sat down in the shade under the wing. I was on the verge of telling him he just wasn't cutting it and maybe he ought to go through the instrument training again - or, maybe, find some other air force occupation.

As I beat around the bush uncomfortably approaching dropping the ax – after all he was a Major and I was just a Lieutenant – I looked up at him. There were tears in his eyes.

"Lieutenant, when I used to fly the fighters, shucks, if we couldn't see where we were goin' there was no need for us to go there."

Geeez! Am I about to end this guy's career? I knew how much I enjoyed flying and this Major evidently wanted it as badly as me. "Major, let's see if we can't dig up a few additional hours of instruction and get you over the hump."

We worked on his problems both in flight and in the ground simulator. Everyone liked the guy and knew he was working hard. He managed to pass his flight check. He graduated and went on into the interceptor phase of training.

Four or five weeks later while making a night approach to the airport in an F-86 in the weather. He crashed and was killed.

I've never forgotten him and I always wondered if I should have . . .

Most of the students who came through the interceptor school were young lieutenants like me, fresh out of flight training. A part of the instrument course was to take them on a cross country flight strictly "on the instruments." They had to plan the entire trip; what altitude to fly, power settings, airspeed, consider the winds aloft and calculate fuel consumption so as to have a proper reserve. The whole flight was done flying instruments terminating in an instrument approach to the landing at the destination.

One of the check points requiring a position report to ground controllers along the way was Tucumcari radio in New Mexico. That name is pronounced "Two – Come – Carry." When we arrived over the radio the student had to check his time over the station with his computed time, make any adjustments, predict his time at the next reporting point and give this information to the operator at Tucumcari Radio.

He called "Too sum marie radio, this is Air Force Jet 12345." There was no answer. He repeated the call to "Too sum marie" radio.

After a short pause this time a voice came back, "Air Force Jet 12345, this is two-come-carry radio, can I help you?"

"No, I'm calling two sum marie radio."

This was followed by another pause. Then a somewhat resigned voice came back: "Air Force Jet 12345, this is too-sum-marie radio. Go ahead with your message."

The rest of the flight went well and we arrived at out destination, Phoenix, without further problems.

Thunderstorms

To aviators everywhere the weather has always presented a problem. And weather forecasters, well, same story. Meteorology, the technical term for "weather guessing," is changing all the time.

During flying training there was no subject that was allotted more instruction time than weather. I have always believed that the reason for all the instruction was that they really weren't that sure about how and why the weather did what it did. They wanted us to know as much about it as we could.

Something else I had noticed was that most weather offices had few windows. There were intimidating rows of teletype machines whirring and clattering and spitting out reports about what the meteorologists at other stations were seeing. The walls were practically papered with charts and tables and drawings and weather maps and long lists of the "winds aloft" at various locations.

When you spoke to the folks working there

they would rub their chins and look thoughtful. Then they would tell you what the weather was doing, what they thought it would do in the future and leave your decision up to you. I sometimes suspected there might be a little witchcraft involved.

I was going to fly one day. One of the things a pilot does before taking off is to get a weather briefing. I had gone to the weather office, flight plan in hand, and gave it to the weather guy. His job included filling out the weather portion of my flight plan.

The weather guy breezily waved his pen in the air and pronounced, "the weather today will be severe clear," and bent down to sign my flight plan.

"Severe clear" I exclaimed! (remember, I told you there were no windows) I pointed toward the door, "Why it's raining cats and dogs out there!" The guy looked up in shocked surprise and headed for the door.

I don't know, maybe it was because I couldn't completely mask the grin on my face. Maybe it was because the guy knew me (we were friends) but he stopped in his tracks, still halfway to the door. He slowly turned and looked at me. I was grinning ear to ear. The sun outside was bright and beautiful. "Get outta here," he retorted. I left but I still had a big grin.

This was in the mid 1950s. Intercontinental ballistic missiles had not yet reached the front page. The military threat we were countering with our interceptors was the Russian Bombers and nuclear bombs.

As I said earlier, weather was always an aviator's problem. Someone in the planning section somewhere got the idea that we, in the interceptors, ought to be able to launch and fly through any kind of weather to counter this threat. This ability, they figured, should also include flying through thunderstorms.

I've gotta tell you a little something about a thunderstorm. They come about because of instability in the atmosphere. A comparison might be to watch the water in a pan heated on a stove. It begins to circulate, rising up and down until it reaches the boiling point. Depending on the amount of heat and the composition of the water it can boil violently enough to overflow the pan. The air circulates in much the same way. A thunbderstorm can have vertical winds moving up and down a hundred miles per hour or more. Moisture forms rain drops which go up with these winds and freeze into hail. They may fall or they may be caught and go up again gaining another layer of ice. Hail up high in clouds can reach the size of baseballs, maybe larger.

When an airplane flies into a thunderstorm the pressure instruments, altimeter, vertical velocity indicator and airspeed indicator become completely useless. A pilot should tighten his safety belt and shoulder harness. When the turbulence and vertical winds hit he just hangs on and tries to maintain something like a level flight attitude. When the hail hits it sounds like a million people with sledge hammers all trying to smash that thin, transparent canopy that surrounds him. A fella's inclined to think back to the last time he went to church. There's nothing for it but to hang on and do the best you can.

This "Thunderstorm Penetration Program" went on for, maybe, two weeks. In that time we had beat the antenna covers off the test aircraft, smashed the aero dynamic contours of the fuselage and the engine intakes and bashed in several sets of wing tanks. Luckily we hadn't lost any aircraft.

They called the program off. None of us objected.

One other brief personal encounter with the mysticism of weather phenomenon and I'll let you go on to other things. I was flying a T-33 single engine jet one night at about 30,000 feet over El Paso, Texas. There were thunderstorms in the area but none very close.

Suddenly there was light outside the ship. I looked up and out and there were three masts of fire extending forward from my aircraft, one from the nose and one on each side from the wing tip fuel tanks. It was St. Elmo's fire, the same stuff that used to terrorize the men aboard sailing ships at sea. It also covered the plexi-glass canopy of the aircraft in a sort of spider web. I put my finger against the inside of the canopy and the fire would follow my finger wherever I moved it. All this had been explained in the many hours of teaching us weather but it was kind of spooky just the same.

"All of us learn to write in the second grade .. most of us go on to greater things."

Bobby Knight

If only I'd have . . .

The interceptor training course was on a schedule with pilots programmed to come and go months in advance. Maintaining the pace of training was important. Sometimes, if we had had a stretch of bad weather, several of us would take the low-time students and fly to another base for a couple days. This kept the schedule on track.

On this occasion there were about eight of us, four instructors and four students in four aircraft scheduled to fly out, as I remember, to Kirtland Air Force Base, Albuquerque, New Mexico. It could have been to a field at Tucson or Phoenix, Arizona. I don't recall. The details don't affect the story.

As we departed Perrin my student and I just happened to be in the lead aircraft – maybe twenty or thirty minutes ahead of the others. The flight went well and the weather at Albuquerque was beautiful, not a cloud in the sky.

Jet aircraft fly at high altitude, higher than piston or turbo prop aircraft for two reasons:

because they can and because a jet engine burns fuel proportionally to the air density. The air is thinner up high, less fuel is burned to attain the same speed and flight range is extended. We had reached Albuquerque and begun our "penetration," our let-down from altitude in anticipation of our approach to land.

While we were enroute two Navy jet fighter aircraft, "Banshee's," F-2H models, had departed Albuquerque heading for El Toro Marine Corp Air Station in California. One of the aircraft encountered a problem. Jet aircraft, because of their high rate of fuel consumption, are often equipped with large supplemental wing tip fuel tanks. In this instance the number two aircraft had been unable to get his left wing tip tank to transfer fuel. Without this fuel he would not be able to reach his destination. Both aircraft elected to return to Kirtland Air Force Base and get the problem repaired.

Fuel in the wing tip tanks places a weight on the wing tip. When landing, unless the tank is empty, that heavy weight on the wing tip can cause damage and in some cases loss of control. The strain on the wing root is like the pressure exerted by a pry bar. The probability of a problem is so great that landing with fuel in wing tip tanks is not recommended.

Navy aircraft had a special feature: they were able to open a valve in each of their wing tip tanks and "dump" the fuel. As these two aircraft approached Albuquerque they began dumping their wing tank fuel in preparation for landing.

The number two aircraft, the one with the original failure of the left wing tip tank to feed, could not get that same left wing tip tank to dump fuel. The lead aircraft – they were a two aircraft flight - elected to go ahead and land. This left his wingman circling the airport alone with his problem.

The problem had been further amplified. With the left tip tank full and the right tip tank empty the aircraft was not in balance. As long as speed was maintained, the aileron controls allowed the pilot to hold the heavy wing up. As the aircraft slowed to land the reduced air speed would not be able to generate sufficient lift to hold the wing up. The wing would stall resulting in a complete loss of control.

With these problems accumulating, the pilot

declared an emergency. This action immediately closed the airport to everyone except the aircraft with the emergency.

We abandoned our own approach. Since we were flying a similarly configured aircraft, a T-33 "shooting star," I began contemplating what I would do under the same circumstances. There were only two choices: attempt to land or bail out.

We were near enough to the airport that we were able to see the Navy aircraft. We stayed well above him and clear of anything he might want to do and followed him.

I thought that, if it were me, I'd try to land. First I'd test my decision at a safe altitude: I'd put the landing gear down, gradually slow the airplane until I was just about to lose control of that heavy wing. Noting that minimum control speed, I'd make a straight-in approach to the runway, keeping just above the loss-of-control airspeed, and attempt to fly the aircraft right onto the runway. At touchdown, if I were able to maintain control, I'd let it roll out until it stopped. If I lost it and it went off the runway or collapsed the landing gear, I'd shut everything down, blow off the canopy, get out of the aircraft and run.

A few more minutes passed in silence. Then the Navy pilot called the tower to tell them he was going to try to land.

Good for you, I thought. I'll keep my fingers crossed.

This guy lined up with the runway – but he was still about 800 feet up in the air – and he wasn't slowing down at all. What the heck is he going to do?

Have you ever seen someone about to do something that was so utterly wrong that you were astounded, utterly amazed that they were doing that? You couldn't believe what you were seeing! Surely they weren't going to . . .

I reached for the throttle. The microphone button was atop the throttle. My thought was to call him and ask what he was doing. Then I thought, no, he's a qualified pilot. He must know what he's doing. Maybe Navy F-2Hs have some special feature – something? Heck, this guy's gonna kill himself! Ben, he's a – he must know – I can't believe what he's about to do.

While I'm arguing with myself the Navy pilot has "pitched out," a normal maneuver when flying a normal traffic pattern for landing. But hey this isn't a normal landing.

During the pitch-out that heavy wing almost caused him do a complete roll instead of just a steep turn. Once again I'm reaching for the microphone button, still arguing with myself.

By now the Navy aircraft has lowered his landing gear and is into another descending turn to align with the runway – a turn right into that heavy wing. My thumb is quivering over the microphone button. Geeezus! This guy is about to die!

And he did.

He wasn't even able to roll out to level flight. That heavy wing stalled. He lost control. The aircraft rolled over and dove into the ground. My thumb is still touching the microphone button. There were several seconds of shocked silence.

Kirtland tower broke the silence. The tower operator called on the radio, "Air Force 12345 is that you over the field?"

I punched the microphone button. "Ah, roger Kirtland, Air Force Jet 12345."

"'45, you're cleared to land. Land long over the wreckage."

Damn!

After we landed I learned that the Navy pilot was still pretty new, just out of flight school. If I had only punched that microphone button and called him, I might not have kept him from killing himself but I could have given him much better odds of survival.

I don't know. Maybe that event was an epiphany or a change of character. Whatever it was you can ask anyone who knows me now, if I've got something to say, you're gonna hear it. I've made a fool of myself from time to time but that hasn't slowed me down a bit. I can still see that guy, out of control and diving into the ground.

The Gift of Wings

Emergency Leave

The policy at Perrin Air Force Base was to try to fly anyone with a genuine emergency, a reason to return home, to a base as near to their destination as we could. There would be a pilot assigned, as an additional duty, to be available even during holidays or weekends to fly such flights should the need arise. I must also say these flights didn't occur often.

The normal sequence of events would be the Red Cross confirming the emergency, Base Operations would be notified, the Aircraft Maintenance section would have an aircraft on standby for just such emergencies and the dispatcher at Base Operations would attempt to contact the assigned duty pilot. This last wasn't always an easy thing. This is where I frequently came in.

I flew aircraft because I loved to fly. I would fly any airplane anywhere at any time unless someone specifically forbade it. I was assigned to the ground school department, teaching in a classroom, and could often get another instructor to "cover" for me – take an assigned class if I had an opportunity to fly.

The dispatchers knew this and would often not even try to search for the duty pilot until they had called me first. I got a good bit of flying that way. I particularly liked these flights because they were always to somewhere different, different weather conditions, different bases at different parts of the country. Each one presented its own challenges and I loved it.

There was one flight – at night. Have you ever noticed how often emergencies happen at night? Anyway, this young airman had an emergency involving his parents who were living in Colorado. When I got to base operations the young fella, a Corporal – that is an "Airman Second Class" by official classification - was already there. For you ex-GIs, he wore two stripes. I checked on the weather and although there were a few clouds along the way there was nothing serious.

His destination had an airport nearby but it wasn't a military field. The closest military base was some eighty miles or so away. The lad's father had had a heart attack, had been rushed to the hospital and was listed in critical condition.

"Young fella, you hang tight. We're gonna get you home."

I calculated my flight plan, double checked fuel requirements, got the latest weather forecast for the destination military field and talked to the weatherman about the probable weather at that nonmilitary field. I think we can do it.

I filed an instrument flight plan to the military field but entered a planned stop at the airman's destination airport. I would, weather permitting, land there, taxi clear of the runway and stop. I would stay in the cockpit with the engine running. The corporal would then climb out of the airplane and be on his way to the hospital. That was the plan.

When we got to the aircraft, prior to climbing in, I briefed this lad again on what we were going to try to do. Even though he had been taught what he needed to know to fly as a passenger in a T-33 jet aircraft, I made doubly sure that he understood what we were going to try and that he knew what to do. He would have to remove and replace the safety pins for the ejection seat, secure the seat belt and shoulder harness after he had climbed out and stay the heck clear of the jet engine intake. If there was a screwup and I was unable to take off from that civilian airstrip again, well, the powers that be would not look kindly upon me.

The flight went well. Weather was pretty much as forecast and we were on time and on my calculated fuel consumption. I was able to contact a navigation radio station operator near our civilian field and he graciously agreed to call a taxi arranging it to pick up my passenger at that empty airport. The radio operator confirmed the taxi had been arranged even though taxi company had been a bit leery about the original request.

Luckily, when we landed the runway lights were on. In the aircraft landing light I could see there was grass growing through the cracks in the runway. Geez! I sure hope we don't have any problems here. I taxied clear of the runway and toward car headlights at the edge of the airport. I was guessing that would be the taxi. Whoever or whatever it was, the young corporal would be on his own once he got out.

I stopped, opened the canopy and passed my passenger my best wishes for him and his father. He thanked me and disconnected from the interphone. I watched him in the rear view mirror as he climbed out of the airplane and off the wing. He waved and headed for those headlights.

I taxied back down the runway, turned, pushed the throttle forward and took off. I was in the air again! We had done it!

I contacted Air Traffic Control, informed them I was back in the air again and was given a route and an altitude to the military airport that was our original destination.

As I reached my assigned altitude I broke out of the clouds. The moon was bright and full - almost silver. Stars seemed so close I could almost touch them, staring down at me from a deep almost black sky. The bright white cloud layer glistened like a silver sea just beneath the wings of my aircraft.

The lines of a poem written by a fellow fighter pilot seemed to drift into my mind of their own accord: ". . . and while with silent lifting mind I've trod the high untrespassed sanctity of space, put out my hand and touched the face of God." I must be doing something right.

The Gift of Wings

Flameout

This was another emergency leave flight and, as usual, it was at night. Why do calls like this always seem to come at night? An airman at Perrin Air Force Base had received word that his father had had a heart attack. His dad was up in Boston. The Corporal was trying to get home as quick as he could on an emergency leave. I guess things didn't look too good for the fella's father.

The CQ (Charge of Quarters) in the officer's barracks came to my room. Lieutenant, you've got a phone call. This was way before the days of cell phones. There was only one phone in the barracks, well, two if you count the pay phone.

"Ben! Could you fly this fella . . . Boston . . . emergency leave . . . heart attack?" It was the dispatcher at Base Operations.

"I'll be right down."

I was still a bachelor living in the Bachelor Officer's Quarters. I was assigned as a ground school instrument instructor, and could often arrange my teaching schedule around these flights. As often as not I would make the flight, return and still be able to teach my classes the next day.

When I arrived at Base Operations the young GI was already there – with a big ole B-4 bag, a sort of suitcase bulging at the seams. We would be flying in a T-33 single engine jet trainer, the two seated training version of the Air Force's first F-80 "Shooting Star" interceptor. The aircraft didn't have space to stow that B-4 Bag but, what the heck, this young fella had troubles enough already. I'd figure out something.

The weather was not the greatest along the route and we'd have to stop at an Air Base in Illinois to refuel. This was nothing we wouldn't be able to handle. When we got into the airplane I had the kid stow his bag crossways on the canopy rails in front of him. He wouldn't be able to see much but it was night and in the weather so there wouldn't be much to see anyway.

After refueling at Scott Air Force Base in Illinois I had to plan on flying a bit south of my desired course because of a row of thunderstorms along the way. No sweat. We could handle that.

Taxiing out for take off I encountered another problem. It was a minor problem but it would return to give me a problem. The red "fuel low" warning light on the instrument panel had stayed in the "on" position.

Let me explain that a little. Jet aircraft eat up fuel like a brand new toilet. They store additional fuel in two sets of wing tanks and a pair of large wing tip tanks, a total of about 813 gallons. The main or fuselage tank only holds about 95 gallons. We would be burning fuel at the rate of about 230 gallons per hour.

That warning light was designed to come on whenever the fuselage tank got low. The pilot would then switch on the fuel pumps from one of the sets of auxiliary tanks. When that set of auxiliary tanks ran out of fuel the fuel level in the fuselage tank would begin to go down. The warning light would come on reminding the pilot to switch to another set of tanks.

The warning light was placed in a prominent position on the instrument panel so it wouldn't be overlooked. With the light stuck in the "on" position and since it was night, dark, it was quite a distraction. I unscrewed the lens and removed the bulb. That took care of that. I made a note, a reminder on my flight log telling me when to switch fuel tanks.

We took off and climbed to our cruising altitude. Since my passenger hadn't received training in flying at high altitude we had to remain below 20,000 feet, down among the airline flights of those days.

Remember that row of thunderstorms I mentioned? Well, the airline pilots had seen them too. Their flight plans avoided those thunderstorms and they were crowded on either side of the thunderstorms. A jet fighter flew faster than those airliners. The Air Traffic Controllers had to keep me and the airliners from conflicting with one another. They found a route that would keep me clear of the airliners: right down through that row of thunderstorms. They called me and gave me my new routing.

What would have been a routine instrument flight suddenly became more complicated. I was folding and unfolding charts to find the new route. I had a pocket sort of a slide rule gadget which was our standard calculator in those days. This was before computers or electronic calculators. I was doing all this while dodging lightning flashes and circumnavigating thunderstorms through the night sky. I was one pretty busy aviator.

I managed to follow the new route while threading my way through all this line of thunderstorms and finally arrived over South Weymouth Naval Air Station, Boston, Massachusetts. And then we had to hold.

Air traffic below wouldn't allow us to come down immediately. I had to position the aircraft over a radio beacon in a race-track type pattern and wait for the Air Traffic Controllers to clear the way for us.

Suddenly the engine quit cold! There was no sputtering or hesitating. One minute it was running, the next it was dead. Do you remember my explaining to you about that "low fuel warning" light? Well, suddenly, I remembered it too. The cockpit lighting dimmed. It got awfully quiet.

I punched the transmit button on the radio. "Boston approach control, be advised that Air Force Jet 1234 has flamed out in the holding pattern. I am descending."

Silence!

"Geezus!" This from my rear seat passenger.

That "low-fuel" warning light was in my pocket. I hadn't noticed the fuselage tank getting low. We had run out of fuel. I quickly switched on another set of fuel tanks hoping that the battery could furnish power enough to operate those fuel pumps. I activated the "Air-Start" ignition. WHOOM! Suddenly the engine was running again.

I keyed the microphone button, "Boston approach control, Air Force Jet 1234, I have restarted. I am at 18,000 feet. Do you want me to maintain 18,000 feet or climb back to 20,000 feet?"

The answer was quicker this time. "Stand by, Air Force Jet 1234." We waited, oh, it couldn't have been more than fifteen or twenty seconds. "Boston approach control clears Air Force Jet 1234 for an immediate approach and landing at South Weymouth Naval Air Station. Call leaving 18,000 feet."

It was pretty much routine from there down to the landing. I taxied along behind the "Follow Me" ramp guide truck to the parking area and shut down the engine.

As we climbed out of the aircraft, my passenger turned to me, white faced, and asked, "Sir? I thought when the airplane flamed-out that that was all there was?"

Well, he had a point there but he also had a father to worry about. I casually replied, "No sweat, son." I inclined my head toward the ramp truck and added, "Jump in the truck and he'll take you to the Main Gate. You can get a cab from there."

My passenger and the ramp truck drove off. I was left standing beside the aircraft on the darkened ramp in the silence. I turned back, closed the canopy, "chocked" the wheels and looked around. There was no sign the ramp truck was coming back for me. About a half mile away I could see lights through the window of one of the blimp hangars. I started walking.

When I arrived at the hangar and let myself in it was apparent that I was in the operations office. A grizzled old Navy Chief Petty Officer was walking around in an office behind the operations counter. He had a cigar stub between his teeth and papers in both hands. He would pause occasionally to dig into a drawer or a file cabinet.

It seemed he hadn't noticed me come in and he looked busy so I waited. Finally, to introduce my presence, I commented, "Looks like you're pretty busy?"

He quickly looked up. "Yeah," he commented around his cigar, "Some son of a ----- flamed out in the holding pattern and I'm trying to figure out who I'm supposed to call."

"Well," I began a little hesitantly, "I was just up there but," I motioned toward the ramp, "I landed and parked and now I'm lookin' for some fuel."

"Was that you? Was that you who flamed out up there?"

I nodded my head.

"Damn! Is everything OK? No problems?"

"Just that I need some fuel so I can get back to Texas."

He threw his papers onto a desk. "OK! Let's just forget about all this. I'll get you some fuel."

The flight back to Texas was at high altitude, clear of the thunderstorms and rather uneventful. I never told anyone about that flame out. The only ones who knew are that Navy Chief and I – and now you know too. Don't tell nobody.

The Radar Approach Hour

A class entering our instrument flight instruction course usually numbered from fifteen to twenty students. Each of us who were instructing the ground school portion of the course had blocks of instruction for which we were the primary instructor. We all had other hours assigned also for which we were the back-up instructor. This was so the school could remain on schedule in case of the incapacity of one person. The system seemed to work well.

I was the primary instructor for, among other things, a one hour class on Radar Ground Controlled Approach, (GCA). I enjoyed flying primarily but, second to that, I enjoyed talking about flying. When a pilot talks to you about flying you will see he uses each hand as if it were an airplane. He'll maneuver and turn and twist. Once you've seen it, you'll recognize it anywhere. I guess I enjoy talking to an audience anyway. So, shoot me.

A ground controlled approach involves several

men in a trailer near the runway equipped with radar. When the weather is bad – I mean really bad – these men can see your aircraft on their radar scopes and give you directions to line you up with the landing runway.

Once you are aligned with the runway and some eight or ten miles away their precision radar scopes can see your aircraft. The controller will talk to you steadily with no breaks. He will give instructions to align the aircraft precisely with the runway. He can also see whether you are descending, in accordance with his instructions, at a rate that will bring the aircraft to the landing zone on the runway.

There are more people involved in a GCA than in other instrument approach systems but it works well. It's kind of reassuring to have another person directly involved in getting you safe onto the ground.

As with any instrument approach there are emergency procedures, procedures to follow if things aren't going right. For a GCA a pilot is informed that if he doesn't hear his controller's voice for fifteen seconds while in the pattern or five seconds while on final approach, "He shall climb to . . ." (Stating whatever the emergency instructions might be.)

In actual practice, while flying in weather requiring a ground controlled approach, a pilot, particularly an all-by-himself fighter pilot, is pretty busy. What to do if he loses contact does not hold that much attraction. Most pilots acknowledge receipt of those emergency procedures with a brief reply: "Roger," indicating he received and understood them. Yeah! And he believes in the Easter Bunny too.

Being aware of this I wanted to impress on the class that there was something they could always do in spite of not remembering those emergency instructions. Each approach has an emergency safe altitude listed. That's an altitude a pilot can climb to that will give him clearance over anything within a twenty five mile radius. If something unforeseen happens, climb to that altitude and figure out what to do next from there.

To accomplish this bit of skill and cunning and to make an impression on the pilots I had orchestrated a part of my instruction.

I would create an intense approach scenario, you know, with "snow capped mountains and shark infested waters." There are ways you're supposed to do instructing and I purposely violated several of them. I used to smoke cigarettes in those days and I would have a cigarette in my mouth, holding it between my teeth and talking around it. I had a piece of chalk in one hand and an eraser in the other. I would give them instructions, simulating they were on an actual approach. I would talk rapidly, make notes on the blackboard and erase them just as quickly. I would also work a rather complicated emergency procedure into my presentation.

Right in the middle of this, usually while simulating the final approach to the runway, I would suddenly stop talking, stop writing, stop doing anything. I would turn back to the class. For several seconds I wouldn't say or do anything. Then I'd ask them, "What do you do now?"

This little stunt never failed to take them completely by surprise. Again I'd ask them, "You've lost communication with GCA. Whaddya gonna do?"

Somebody might remember some part of the emergency procedures and might blurt it out. No one ever remembered all of what they were instructed to do. And that response was so true to actual life. That's when I'd plug the emergency safe altitude. Climb to the emergency safe altitude and figure out what to do next.

Well, I was in the middle of one of these presentations one day. I had been polishing my presentation and working on it for several classes. Modesty prevents me from saying I was good at it but I was good at it. Right in the middle, cigarette between my teeth, chalk writing and eraser erasing, I glanced back at the class.

Every darn one of those twenty or so students was leaning forward, sitting on the edge of their seats, hanging on every word I said. That sight startled me so badly that I forgot where I was in the presentation and blew the whole thing. When they realized what had happened we all had a laugh.

I guess a little humility is a good thing.

C-47 "Skytrain" Transport

The Desperate Time

How much of what you think is real - - and how much is "just in your head?"

I have a daughter-in-law who, when she crosses the Mackinac Bridge connecting Michigan's Upper and Lower Peninsula, has to get someone else to drive the car. She experiences a sort of panic attack. This situation is so common the bridge has personnel that routinely provide a driver for those who have this problem. Maybe you know someone who suffers from a similar anxiety? To them the fear is real. To the rest of us "it's all in their head."

Most Air Force Bases had one or more C-47 "Skytrain" transport airplanes assigned. They were used like you might use your pickup truck, for hauling one thing or another from here to there. The C-47 is an "old faithful" reliable aircraft. It is sometimes affectionately called "The Gooney Bird" after those resident birds on Midway Island. The civilian designation for the C-47 is the DC-3. It was originally built by Douglas Aircraft

Company back in the early 1930s. The British use the aircraft also and dubbed it the "Dakota."

The DC-3 was a gigantic leap forward in the transport aircraft of the day. The fact that it is still around is a testament to its rugged construction and dependability.

There were a couple C-47 cargo aircraft assigned to Perrin Air Force Base. They were used for flying groups of people from one place to another or to pick up or deliver cargo.

There wasn't a full-time C-47 pilot assigned. There were a group of us who were checked out to fly the airplane. The group was large enough that, even though the members had other primary duties, there was enough flexibility among us that a pilot and copilot could be found when needed. For some of us it presented another opportunity to fly and gave us experience in a different aircraft. For others it was a matter of "filling squares."

In addition to the standard military pay scale there was what was called "flight pay." Actually the official term was "hazard pay." To qualify for this pay a person had to have flown at least four hours that month. Overall, and I'm guessing here but I'm sure I'm close to being correct, to remain rated as a pilot the person had to have flown a minimum of 100 hours each year. They also had to pass their annual flight check and their flight physical examination. The C-47 required a pilot and copilot so we who were checked out as pilots were often called upon to fill in as copilot also. For me, what the heck, it was flying. There were some of us who were getting a good bit of flying time and some who, because of circumstances or often by design, were only interested in getting the minimum.

Being a bachelor I probably spent more time at the bar in the officer's club than many of the others. I would have a drink of something potent now and then but mostly it was softer drinks. The attraction of the bar was the company, the socializing and the conversation. I probably downed a whole lot of soda pop in my time.

I guess pilots are a lot like fishermen in that the stories they tell might be – how can I put this – might be a little "embellished." It was a popular pastime to relate "war stories," tales of adventures in the air which were traded back and forth. It brings to mind the expression, "The first liar doesn't stand a chance."

A story was circulating among the C-47 pilots of a pretty wild adventure by one of the group. It seems he had been sent to pick up a High School choral group down in Houston. They would be coming to the Perrin area to entertain at some sort of celebration.

He landed at Houston and the choral group wasn't there. They had been delayed. He had to wait for the group to be bussed to the airport. He finally got them loaded aboard. It was late afternoon when he took off to return to Perrin.

The weather had deteriorated during his delay at Houston and thunderstorms were developing north of Dallas in the Perrin area. It was getting dark. He could see lightning flashes ahead on his route of flight.

He called the radar site at Perrin but they were no help. They couldn't identify him among the thunderstorms. The only radio navigation aid he had available was the low frequency radio range receiver. In clouds and/or with thunderstorms and lightning about all a person would hear on that low frequency was static.

The automatic direction finding feature of the low frequency receiver was more apt to point to the lightning flashes than to a ground radio beacon. It was beginning to sound like "sweat-city," especially with a load of teen age kids aboard.

He considered landing at Dallas but the schedule for their singing was yet that evening. "Snow capped mountains and shark infested waters" was the popular way of describing his predicament. Finally, through skill and cunning and deeds of derring-do, he was able to land them safely at Perrin. They boarded a waiting bus and were whisked off to their engagement on time and in good order thanks to the superb skill and ability of their pilot. Cheers, congratulations and drinks all around!

As I heard this story repeated for the ninth or tenth time I began to recognize little features of that flight. As you all are probably aware, stories like that tend to be high on the almost and darn near scale. Nailing down facts can be a whole 'nother matter.

After a little digging I was able to identify the date and place of the flight, the particular pilot involved and – low and behold – I had been his copilot on that flight.

My recollection was similar to his except for the "snow capped mountains and shark infested waters" part. When we returned to Perrin it was evening but not yet dark. There were scattered thunderstorms in the area but nothing we couldn't easily fly around and avoid. Perrin radar was not completely up and running – some sort of maintenance - at the time and couldn't help us. We just flew in a northerly direction from Dallas until we contacted Perrin's Ground Controlled Approach radar, the precision approach radar, who talked us down to a landing.

My recollection of the flight in question was that it was no big deal. To the guy who was flying the pilot's seat though, he was one of the "four hours a month and minimum annual flight time" group, it was an adventure. This doesn't make me brave and fearless and him a coward. I can get just as scared as anyone else but, to him, in his mind, he was in real danger.

I used to listen, wide eyed to stories like this. My thought was that if things like that happened to folks who fly, why, it was only a matter of time before something like that was going to happen to me. What would I do?

Over in Southeast Asia where we were shooting at one another, the bar in the officer's club did an active business. The chaplains usually had a full house on Sunday. Those chaplains use to be in the club also having a drink "with the troops."

Frequently you might notice an individual, sitting alone, drink in hand and staring away off into the distance. Barroom humor called this "the fifty mission stare" The guys condition would be referred to as "too many too close for too long."

I'm not a psychiatrist. I can't tell you for sure but maybe that C-47 pilot with his large accumulation of flying hours had experienced "too many too close for too long." He flew the airplane well, made a good approach and landing. All I did on that flight was ride the right seat and lower the landing gear when he called for it. That was the copilot's task.

I'm not trying to be the other guy's "judge and jury." Maybe many of you know people whose imaginations can create problems where no problems exist. Who really knows what goes on in another person's head?

"They patch 'er up with paper clips

With bailing wire, with string.

She always flies, she nefer dies,

Methuselah, with wings"

A fond ode to the C-47, the DC –3, "The Gooney Bird" by the men who have flown her.

The first model of what would to become Douglas Aircraft's DC-3 "Skytrain" first flew in 1933.

A testament to the soundness and reliability of this aircraft is the fact that many are still flying today and flown by pilots less than half as old as the aircraft.

Midway Island in the Pacific

Ice and Snow

This is another C-47 "Skytrain" story. Let me tell you a little something about this aircraft. If they gave medals to aircraft surely the C-47 – one of its pet names is "the goony bird" named after the albatross's that live on Midway Island in the Pacific – should be awarded about as many as the old bird could carry. Other designations for the same aircraft are: the civilian DC-3 Dakota, the Navy R-4D, the troop carrier version the "Skytrooper" and "Puff, the Magic Dragon" or

"Spooky" for the gunship version used in Viet Nam.

The airplane was built by Douglas Aircraft with the first one taking to the air December 17th 1935. They're still being flown by almost all nations in all parts of the world. Most pilots these days are flying this aircraft which was designed and built before they were born. Its durability and longevity testify to the quality of its construction.

"They patch 'er up with paper clips, with bailing wire and string. She always flies. She never dies – Methuselah with wings."

I love that old airplane.

Anyway I caught a flight to Salt Lake City, Utah, to pick up some cargo. There are load limits, maximum take off weights, restrictions like that are a part of any aircraft operation manual. For anyone interested the history of the C-47 is unbelievable in the things it has done, the loads it has carried. Over in Asia it has even hauled livestock, cattle. I was never told who cleaned up after them but I imagine some poor suffering crew chief knows the drill.

This flight didn't involve any overloads. It

was just a routine pick-up-some-cargo flight. At Salt Lake there were delays. You get used to it. There always seem to be delays. By the time we filed our flight plan it was night and there was weather over the mountains. I chose the northern route back to Texas flying the airways over the mountains.

Airways are like freeways for airplanes. They have been surveyed; they run from radio fix to radio fix. They are about ten miles wide (it varies) and have a minimum altitude for safe flight published on the chart. This is necessary to keep the aircraft above obstacles along the way.

The C-47 aircraft ceiling, the maximum altitude it can fly, is about 24,000 feet. Twelve thousand feet is the maximum altitude for people without supplemental oxygen.

The minimum altitude for the airway across the mountains was 17,000 feet. Salt Lake itself is about 4,200 feet above sea level so we would have to climb an additional 13,000 feet to get to that minimum altitude. There's a reason for my explaining all this. You just hang in there.

In addition to me, my copilot and the crew chief, we picked up a hitch hiker at Salt Lake.

This was an Army guy heading home on leave. He wasn't going where we were going but our destination, Perrin, would get him a whole lot closer than Salt Lake.

We took off into the clouds and weather. Radar departure control cleared us to "climb on course." Waaait a minute here! Climb on course? It's dark and we're in the clouds. There are mountains "on course." I don't think so. We had better circle and climb a bit before proceeding "on course." I made the request. They nonchalantly OK'd it.

There's a lesson here for young pilots. Those guys on the ground are good fellas but there's a reason they call you the Aircraft Commander. You're the one in command.

We circled once and proceeded on our way.

The higher a person climbs in the air, the colder the temperature gets. The rate is something like three degrees cooler for each thousand feet of altitude. We had to go to 17,000 feet. It was cold up there.

Clouds are visible moisture, water, just like you see coming from a boiling kettle. The water in clouds can become "super-cooled." That's when water cools below its freezing point but remains liquid - until it is "disturbed." Flying through a cloud "disturbs" this super-cooled water. Ice then begins to form on the airplane.

It's not the weight of ice forming on an airplane that creates a problem. The wings, the flying surfaces and the propellers of an airplane are precisely designed in accordance with Bernoulli's principle. Bernoulli discovered that by increasing the velocity of air it causes a decrease in pressure and temperature. This pressure decrease on the top of the wing creates the lift by which the airplane flies. The same principle applies to the propeller which is a "wing" also. Ice forming on these surfaces can change their shape destroying their ability to create lift.

So here we come at 17,000 feet through these super-cooled clouds. Being knowledgeable aviators we are watching in case ice begins to form. It does. Ice first becomes apparent on the windscreen and on the wings. Our aircraft is equipped with de-icing boots. The leading edge of each wing is covered in a rubber bladder containing three rubber tubes. When the boots are turned on, air pressure alternates into and out of each of these boots causing them, in turn, to expand, then contract. It's important to let the ice build up before turning the boots on. The boots will crack formed ice, not prevent ice building up. In fact, if the boots are left on and the icing is heavy, the ice will form around the pulsating boots. Bad news.

When the propellers ice up they too grow less efficient. The airspeed indicator will show a loss of airspeed. Airspeed slowing down and wing ice building up is a sort of "coffin-corner." You don't want to go there.

For the propeller icing problem there is an alcohol tank just behind the pilot's seat. An electric pump sends the alcohol out through a tube to a slinger ring which spins with the propeller. Separate tubes in the slinger ring end in nozzles at each propeller blade. The alcohol is "slung" through these nozzles to run out along the leading edge of each propeller blade washing the ice off.

Now, we, in our C-47, are about to do battle with the demon airfoil icing. There's another battle condition here that is important. You remember my telling you a human needed oxygen above 12,000 feet? Well, we're at 17,000 feet.

We don't have oxygen masks but there is oxygen aboard the aircraft and a sort of rubber hose in the cockpit. The copilot and I casually pass that oxygen hose back and forth, taking a suck on it occasionally.

We each look out at the leading edge on the wings and turn the boots on. When the ice cracks free we turn them off again. So goes the war.

The alcohol pump is turned on and is "washing" the propellers. We know that's working because the ice being washed off the propellers is slung off and outward. Some of it hits the fuselage of the aircraft sounding a lot like someone is firing buckshot at us.

All seems to be going well except that the icing conditions are persisting for longer than we anticipated. Pretty soon we no longer hear the propeller ice hitting the side of the airplane. The airspeed begins to slow down.

I holler back to the crew chief. He comes up to the cockpit and I quickly brief him on our problem. In the meantime we are still turning the de-icing boots on and off.

The crew chief, God bless him, had an extra container of alcohol in the back of the airplane.

He takes the cap off the tank just behind my seat. We're passing that oxygen hose around among three of us now and we're sucking more often because we're working harder. The smell of the alcohol, some of which gets spilled, is not helping the situation at all. The airspeed continues to fall.

About the time the chief gets the cap back on the alcohol tank and we turn the pump on, that big bird sort of shudders and drops maybe four hundred feet in altitude. As soon as I feel it stalling I push the nose forward to "break" the stall and to regain a little of that lost airspeed.

There are four sets of very large and "scared" or "concerned" - you pick your own description - eyeballs in that cockpit. Yes, I said FOUR sets of eyeballs. Between the time the ship shuddered 'til I recovered our Army passenger was up to the cockpit too.

Fortunately the propeller ice began bouncing off of the fuselage again, the airspeed came back up and shortly we were past the mountains. As soon as it was feasible I requested and was given clearance to descend to a lower – and a warmer – altitude. Icing was no longer a problem.

The rest of the flight was pretty much normal. By now it was the wee hours of the morning. The copilot and I talked about darn near everything we could think of to keep each other awake until we were able to land back at Perrin Air Force Base – and to bed.

This isn't quite the end of the story though. It had to have been a year or two later when I was on another flight. I was walking through the operations office at a base in Illinois when I heard a voice calling me. I turned around but it took a minute or two before I located a fella waving and calling to me. Can you guess who it was? It was that Army fella who almost fell into the Rocky Mountains with me that night. I guess that was a flight to remember.

The Gift of Wings

Get Home-itis

K.I. Sawyer Air Force Base was located in Michigan's Upper Peninsula at Gwinn, very near to my hometown, Marquette. North Central Airlines was providing an airline connection at the field before the Air Force came in.

North Central flew the twin engine DC-3 "Skytrain" (This is the same aircraft the military called the C-47 "Gooneybird"). It was and still is a safe, sound, reliable old bird and is currently flying in all corners of the world. North Central's "logo" I guess you'd call it was a silhouette of a goose, wings upraised, in dark blue paint on the tail assembly. That gained the company and its aircraft another fond and affectionate moniker; "the Blue Goose".

When the military first selected Sawyer to be an Air Force Base I wrote to my dad in Marquette. I told him that when the base became activated I would be able to fly up on the occasional weekend and visit.

The Air Force sent Lieutenant Colonel

Stanley Long, a local Marquette fella, to be the acting Base Commander. He was in charge of a skeleton crew of men preparing the way for the expansion. My father was the Assistant Chief of the Marquette Police Force and knew Stan Long. He picked up the telephone, called him, told him what I had said.

The Colonel told him that even though the base was not yet operational they did have starting units and could provide gasoline.

Jet aircraft can burn gasoline although it burns hotter and faster than recommended jet fuel. They could provide enough gasoline to get me over to Kinross Air Force Base (later named Kinchloe Air Force Base) near Sault Ste. Marie, Michigan. They could provide jet fuel there.

The opportunity to fly home came, I planned the flight, jumped in the cockpit of a T-33 and was on my way to K.I. Sawyer Air Force Base.

The weather at Sawyer was forecast to be a little iffy and Sawyer didn't yet have a published instrument approach. Kinross Air Force Base wasn't very far from Sawyer so I had planned to go to Kinross if things didn't work out.

In jets, fuel is always a prime consideration

and I was working with the minimum for this flight. Since there was no published radio aid for Sawyer, I found the antenna location for the WDMJ, the Marquette area's local broadcast radio station, and plotted and measured the heading and distance from it to Sawyer. This wouldn't be an instrument approach but it would help me find the airport if things were a little questionable. The thing is, I wanted to get home for a visit.

It was dark when I arrived "in the area" of K.I. Sawyer Air Force Base. I say "in the area because, as I said, there were no radio navigation aids there. Luckily I was above a cloud layer, not in it, and the automatic direction finding capability of my older low frequency radio receiver was working. I flew to the local broadcast radio station antenna,

I turned over that antenna, took up my preplanned heading. With the distance already measured and knowing the speed at which I was flying I knew how many minutes and seconds before I was over Sawyer – hopefully.

I flew out the time, rolled the wing up and looked down. Nothing! My heart sank as I anticipated having to fly on to Kinross.

There was a cloud layer below me and, it being night, everything was black. The clouds were reported as "broken" which meant there were holes here and there. Just as I was about to head over to Kinross I spotted two rows of lights through a hole in the clouds.

That must be the runway! Hooray! I've found Sawyer. I rolled over, throttled back and dove for that hole in the clouds.

As I got lower, through that hole, I could see more. Wait a minute? Those two rows of lights are turning! An airport runway doesn't turn! It's gotta be straight. Geez! If I've let down and now have to climb back up again, I might not have fuel enough to . . wait! Wait a minute!

Suddenly, below the clouds now, I could see an even wider area. Those lights I had seen were illuminating the roadway from the highway into the air base. There were the runway lights right over there, straight and true and bright. I loved those lights.

I swung around in a tight turn, dropped the aircraft landing gear and set 'er down on that beautiful long, straight, lighted runway.

After landing the only lighted building I could

see was behind me, where I had initially touched down. I turned and taxied back, turning off on the taxiway that led to the lighted building. The ramp area was clear and I was able to turn around again, pulled up and stopped about two hundred feet or so from the little building.

Some guy was standing in the lighted doorway, hands in his pockets and leaning against the door jam.

I looked at him looking at me and thought, "Hey, an airplane has just arrived. You're supposed to meet it. You know, wave your arms to direct it, point, things like that."

Nothing! The two of us just looked at one another. Then a pickup truck came racing across the airfield. As it got closer I recognized the familiar outline of a standard air force "follow-me" ramp truck. The driver turned on the lights of the sign over the rear of his cab. "FOLLOW ME" This was more like it.

I followed the truck back across the runway to the Air Force side of the field. The truck stopped and the guy jumped out with two flashlight "wands" which he waved and pointed and directed me where to park. Now this was more like it. I felt like I was home – and I was. After all the wandering and wondering I was home for the weekend.

The story is not quite over. I had to partially fuel up with gasoline and fly over to Kinross to fill up for the flight back to Texas.

I had to leave on Sunday to be back at Perrin Air Force Base for work by Monday morning. With the stop at Kinross too, I had to leave early.

Jet aircraft were still pretty new things, especially in Michigan's Upper Peninsula. Many of the folks had never seen one. And I was here with one, the firstest with the mostest.

With internal fuel tanks filled with gasoline I had enough fuel for "a little fooling around." The wing tip tanks being empty reduced the aircraft weight by almost a ton and a half making the bird a little perky. The weather was good, clear skies and sunshine. I took off – and headed for Harvey, where my folks lived, just south of Marquette. I came across that country area as fast as that little ole bird would go and then pulled straight up, climbing two or three thousand feet in less time than it takes to tell it. I did rolls and loops and vertical recoveries and most everything I could think of. The ole airplane fell into a couple maneuvers I didn't know what they were but I tried to put on the best show I could before I had to head out to Kinross.

None of this was done over a populated area and I was careful not to fly below the legal altitude but the roar of that jet evidently attracted a pretty good audience.

Later, when the Air Force Thunderbirds put on their precision acrobatic show at the base opening, several of our neighbors commented to my sister, "Your brother put on a better show than that." I truly didn't come anywhere near competing with the Thunderbirds but I was first! That counts for something!

A little aside here, for whatever it's worth. I landed at K.I. Sawyer Air Force Base the night of the 23rd of October, 1956. The base was not yet open. There would be an official opening, dignitaries would fly in, there would be a ceremony, aircraft fly-bys, speeches made and notations entered in the Base Historians log commemorating "the first flight into K, I, Sawyer Air Force Base."

But I know - and now you do too - that I was the first guy to land an Air Force jet aircraft at Sawyer Air Force Base.

Make a note of that. With that bit of knowledge – and a dollar or so – you'll be able to get a cup of coffee at most any restaurant anywhere.

Strategic Air Command

The cold war seemed to be heating up. General Curtis LeMay was expanding Strategic Air Command. The male fist of SAC's logo reached out and grabbed me.

The Air Force, like businesses everywhere, is divided into specialties. Air Training Command,

ATC, was involved in training. Air Defense Command, ADC, controlled the early warning radar sites and the interceptor aircraft (The interceptor jockeys we had been training at Perrin Air Force Base for instance), Strategic Air Command, SAC, was charged with destroying an enemy's ability to support his war machine, Air Material Command, well, you get the idea. And, of course, every now and then the whole system is rearranged in the interest of efficiency or whatever.

I was transferred from Perrin Air Force Base in Texas to McConnel Air Force Base at Wichita, Kansas. There were B-47 jet bombers there, "Stratojets.". They were powered by six jet engines on swept-back wings, streamlined with "roller-skate" landing gear: a pair of wheels under the nose and another pair further aft under the fuselage. There were also a couple spindly outriggers for balance. It was a truly beautiful aircraft but a deadly beauty. It was designed to carry nuclear bombs, the big ones. This was serious business.

When SAC brings personnel into its command they conduct exhaustive background checks.

FBI agents showed up in my home town asking questions about me. It was enough to make some folks think I might have committed some great crime or something. With a war plan involving deep penetration of enemy territory and tremendously destructive weapons they had to have reliable people.

Talking about war and killing people in a mass destruction is one thing. Seeing it and taking part in it is quite another. The people who make the decisions, who decide to go to war ought to have had some personal experience with – well - I'd better stay away from the politics of these things.

Along with training in the mechanics of the aircraft, the fuel systems, the flight characteristics, dropping bombs and radiation hazards we also had to learn to operate as a team, a three man crew.

At this time I had only attained the rank of First Lieutenant. Nevertheless – I guess it must have been my flying experience – I was to be trained as the Air Craft Commander. My copilot was also a First Lieutenant. My navigator was a Major. We were a good crew. The navigator and I got along well. We each had our specialty and each respected the other fella's turf but the flight decisions were mine. The copilot never did completely agree with his status but he did a good job and I didn't feel I could ask for more than that.

It took me a little time to get used to a "crew" arrangement. I had spent my flying career, up to here, making all the decisions myself. I now had a staff.

There was a block of instruction that had been pilot-labeled the "Navigator Appreciation Course." Up to here our navigation had been by radio aids and/or by ground radar assistance. For flights of the length these larger aircraft flew, across oceans and arctic areas, for example, some other form of navigation was required. Later there would be "inertial navigation" and later yet would come the global positioning system. Back in these days we were still relying on celestial navigation, not so far removed from that used by Christopher Columbus.

Let me give you a brief understanding of the principle of celestial navigation. I'm going to talk about stars now, not planets. Planets are a whole 'nother thing. The basis is that the stars are stationary in relation to each other and to the earth. The earth rotates and moves around the sun but there's a manual that contains corrections for that so stick with the stars.

In celestial navigation stars in the night sky are seen as stationary, like the light in the center of your living room. And with a star, just as the light in your living room, if you have to look straight up to see it you know you are directly under it. The angle you have to look up is called the "altitude" of the star (light). If there are two ceiling lights, their direction and the altitude can be compared and you have a pretty good idea where you are. If there's a third light you are able to determine your position even more exactly. There are a lot of holes in that explanation but you get the idea.

A navigator may describe the exactitude of his calculated position, referring to it as "a three star fix." Cynical pilots often retort, "Yeah, 'three star fix,' 'Deneb' (a very bright star), 'Dubhe' (the star that is the lip of the big dipper) and 'Dallas' (the navigator peeking out the window at the town in Texas)."

We had our ups and downs through the training

but we gradually melded together and became a crew. Modesty prevents my saying so but, if I weren't so modest, I'd say we were one of the best.

Down the road the copilot and I did reach a point where a decision had to be made. I told him he was doing an excellent job but that we had to get together on who was who. He said that we had to have an agreement. I said we did have an agreement. He was the copilot and I was the aircraft commander. I was getting a little short of patience and I added, "When I say 'jump,' you jump!"

This guy was a Naval Academy Graduate, Annapolis, while I was a "Mustang," an officer who had worked his way up through the ranks.

There were just the two of us when this confrontation took place so there should have been no long-term embarrassment. I was a little afraid I might have made the situation worse but he evidently thought about it, accepted the situation and we did go on to make an excellent crew. In fact we were rated in the top ten percent of all SAC combat crews.

B-47 "Sratocruiser"
One of the most beautiful aircraft ever built.

Electronic Counter Measures

Crews were formed up at McConnel Air Force Base. A pilot-copilot combination was put together early in the training. These two strangers to each other had to learn to operate the aircraft systems together and, basically, learn to fly the airplane; to take off and land and, importantly, to rely on each other.

For an ex-fighter pilot this took a lot of doing but, on the other hand, the B-47 was a lot of airplane.

Later in the training the navigators and their bases of assignment were listed in a notice on the bulletin board. We pilots mostly chose the base we wanted to go to since we hadn't yet met the navigators.

Being a First Lieutenant I was probably the most junior Aircraft Commander in the class which meant I probably wouldn't have a whole lot of choice. However it was decided the end result was that we, my copilot and I, crewed up with a navigator, a Captain, who was assigned to Lockbourne Air Force Base near Columbus, Ohio. That base was later named Rickenbacker Air Force Base and as of this writing is Rickenbacker International Airport. So much for the details.

Lockbourne was home to the 376th Bomb Wing and the 301st Bomb Wing. These two B-47 Wings were partners in an Electronic Counter Measures mission. My crew – I refer to it as "my crew" because I was in fact the commander - was assigned to the 25th Bomb Squadron, 376th Bomb Wing.

They called us "Bomb Squadron" and "Bomb Wing" because those were the aircraft we flew.

We didn't carry any bombs. We carried a bomb bay filled with electronic transmitters.

I'm going to wander a bit from the "flying" stories here. You may remember that I worked in electronic counter measures, ECM, as a maintenance man back at Carswell Air Force Base in Fort Worth. I rose to the rank of Staff Sergeant in that job. Well now I am a lieutenant and an aircraft commander in a B-47 bomber and I'm back in the ECM business.

Electronic Counter Measures is a fascinating field. I spent the years from about 1958 until some time in 1963 with Electronic Counter Measures in the B-47. If you'll bear with me I'd like to tell you a little bit about what we were doing.

In World War II, when Germany was bombing London, their problem was finding London. They didn't fly much in daylight because the Royal Air Force Fighter Command made it extremely uncomfortable. When they attacked at night, the British would turn the lights off. The Germans built a radio station that transmitted a beam from occupied France directly over London. Now they could fly over London but when would they release their bombs?

The Germans set up another radio further down the coast and beamed it over London also. Now the bombers could fly out one beam until they intercepted the other – then "Bomb's Away!"

The British weren't asleep during all this. They too set up a radio on the same frequency as that second German radio. They sent their beam to intercept that first German beam somewhere out over open land.

The British also had radar sites along their coast. They referred to them as the "Chain Home" system. It would detect incoming German bombers and better utilize their slim fighter aircraft resources.

The Germans got wise to this, tried to blow up the ground sites and also started dumping "chaff," also called "window." Chaff was thin strips of tin foil cut to a length to reflect radar waves that would "fool" the radar by indicating many more targets, German Bombers, than there actually were.

When people on either side were trying to communicate with each other, their opponent would "jam" their radio. They would do this by transmitting another radio signal in some cases sending the noise from a microphone out in the aircraft engine nacelle, the roar of the engine. "Oh, I say, that must have been a jolly good time, eh, what?"

There have been a lot of improvements, if we can call them that, since those World War II days. Russia was now the threat. The interceptor business I had involved with been back at Perrin trained pilots to shoot down incoming bombers, should the need arise. I was now to be one of the bombers - flying into Russia.

Our sister wing, the 301ˢᵗ Bomb Wing, had B-47s which had been modified to carry a pressurized compartment in their bomb bays. Two Electronic Counter Measures operators would be in that compartment along with oscilloscopes and receivers and controlling transmitters. We would penetrate an enemy's territory in a spread formation three or four miles wide. There would be a 376ᵗʰ aircraft in each outboard position "barrage" jamming. The two 301ˢᵗ aircraft would be in the two inboard positions. These inboard ECM operators would listen and watch the activity on their 'scopes. Their job would be to "spot" jam any enemy signal that attempted to overpower our jamming.

There were classified flights, aptly called "Ferret" flights that regularly patrolled the hostile perimeter – sometimes penetrating into hostile territory. Their task was to determine, monitor and record hostile defensive measures. This information would be fed to us to preset our transmitters to counter the specific threat.

Guys were shot down flying these missions but they were determined to be a necessary thing. You all didn't read much about that in your newspapers but it was happening.

Here's another tidbit that was never included in news releases: a thing the F-86 pilots referred to as "the twenty-fifth rocket." There was only a single hour in ground school devoted to this subject. Typically the instructor would set it up this way.

"Suppose the war has started. The battle for North America is underway. You are stationed on the East Coast (of the United States). You have been launched, intercepted your target, fired all twenty four rockets and shot it down. You're now returning to base with an empty rocket pod. The ground controller calls you. There is one more bomber, nuclear armed, heading for New York City. The only aircraft between that bomber and the people of New York City is you."

Your rocket pod is empty. Watcha gonna do?

Ground radar can set you up for an intercept. Your airborn radar will steer you to a firing position – with nothing to fire.

There's a switch on your armament panel. It's covered by a red safety guard that's safety wired down. If you break that safety wire, raise the guard and turn on that switch it will remove the "lead collision" ballistics from your attack computer. The computer will now steer you on a collision course.

Nobody asks but the question is left hanging there. Watcha gonna do?

It tends to be awfully quiet at the bar that evening, each man sitting alone with his thoughts.

Next time you see some guy – or gal these days – in a uniform, remember these little insights I've given you.

One more little bit and I'll quit, move on to other stories.

The "War Plan" had us in the ECM business penetrating hostile territory at high altitude to cover as much area with our jamming as we could. The bombers, the boys with the nuclear weapons, would be penetrating along with us. The planners determined that the bombers stood a better chance for a successful penetration if they descended to a low altitude – a <u>very low</u> altitude. They would be flying, for the most part, under enemy radar. What about us in the ECM birds? The expression that covers that situation tends to be "alone, unarmed – and darn scared."

Milk – on the Windscreen

This happened during a flight out of Lockbourne Air Force Base. To stay sharp in our ability to carry the threat to the enemy we flew regular training missions. We were required to meet scheduled take off times within +/-:03 minutes. We practiced rendezvousing with tanker aircraft for in-flight refueling, navigating over long distances and simulated bombing runs. On the navigation legs we used celestial navigation using stars, planets and/or the sun. These were viewed in azimuth and elevation through a sextant at precisely calculated times. The measurements and computations were then used to determine where we were and where we were going.

This day we were flying the celestial navigation segment of a mission. These navigation legs were pretty boring for the pilot. The copilot gets involved with taking the celestial observation for the navigator occasionally. Mostly both of us just monitor the aircraft and engine instruments and systems. The automatic pilot drives the aircraft.

Sometimes, depending on the individuals involved, we'd play little jokes on one another to break the monotony.

On this particular flight we were at thirty some thousand feet (seven miles up in the air) flying the celestial navigation leg of our assigned mission. The aircraft interior was pressurized down to an altitude of about 8,000 feet both for the comfort and the efficiency of the crew.

The navigator's position was up in the nose of the aircraft doing the things that navigators do. The copilot and I were just sort of basking in the sunshine coming through the transparent canopy and trying to stay awake.

Impulsively I reached down and pulled the cabin depressurization handle. Cabin pressure shot up to thirty some thousand feet. This sudden release of pressure, the expansion, caused the air to cool. Moisture in the air condensed and fog filled the cockpit.

The navigator immediately keyed the intercom, his voice a couple octaves above normal, asking what had happened. When he heard the copilot and me giggling he knew what we had done. I reset the handle. The cabin re-pressurized and we all returned to what we had been doing.

A little later in the flight the navigator was taking a break to eat his in-flight lunch. The flight lunch included one of those half-pint "box" containers of milk. Looking at that milk carton he got an idea of his own.

The navigator has a sextant port just over his head. This allows him, by opening the sextant port, to push a sextant through it and take his own celestial observations. This sextant port happens to open up just in front of the pilot's windscreen.

The navigator opened the top of the milk carton completely. He held the open mouth of the milk carton up to his sextant port. Then he opened the port to the outside. Cabin pressure immediately crushed the milk carton forcing the milk to erupt through that sextant port like a volcano.

My windshield suddenly went pure white! I couldn't see a thing forward. I grabbed the controls, checked the instruments and tried to figure out what had happened. Then I heard the navigator giggling. Revenge is sweet.

At the altitude we were flying the temperature was about forty degrees below zero. That milk froze solid immediately upon hitting the windshield. We flew the rest of the mission with a "white-out" over my windshield.

When we got back to Lockbourne Air Force Base we made the standard rapid jet let-down for landing. The milk on the windshield did not, as we had expected, melt and run off – it sublimated. The frozen milk turned from ice to vapor leaving the white on the windshield. I couldn't see forward for landing. What to do?

The navigator opened his sextant port and tried to splash some water out but, without the assistance of pressure in the aircraft, it wasn't working.

While we were wondering what to do the co-pilot called Columbus Approach Control. This was the civilian radar operator, located at Port Columbus Airport, who controlled and directed all approaches including those to Lockbourne. "Do you have any rain showers in the area," the copilot asked? "Why, yes," the controller replied, "we have numerous rain showers in the area."

"Could you vector us through a rain shower please?"

"Roger. Take up a heading of zero-nine-zero

degrees for 13 miles."

We did. After a bit of silence, the controller, his curiosity obviously getting the better of him, asked, "Uh, Air Force Jet XXX, why did you want to fly through a rain shower?"

The copilot came back quick as a flash, "We want to wash the milk off the windshield." This was followed by another period of silence.

Once more the controller keyed his microphone, "Aah, Air Force Jet XXX, how did you get milk on your windshield?"

Not missing a beat the copilot responded, "We hit a cow." That was the end of the conversation.

We continued on, washed the windscreen in the rain shower and then landed at Lockbourne.

Looking back on it I couldn't help wondering what that approach controller thought of all that.

The Gift of Wings

The Cuban Missiles

For years Strategic Air Command had a Combat Alert program. A certain number of aircraft were always manned and loaded and ready to go to war. They were preflighted daily, heavily guarded, and parked on a section of the ramp near the runway. Combat crews and ground crew were constantly assigned to each of these aircraft. These "alert crews" were on duty 24 hours a day for periods of up to a week or more. They lived in barracks near the planes.

The War Planning Staff, evaluating enemy capabilities, had determined that an enemy missile launch would only allow, depending on Base location, from 15 to 25 minutes of early warning. That's how much time we had to get our strike force into the air.

There were warning klaxons around the base that would sound whenever the command post signaled an alert. Aircrews and ground crews would rush to their assigned aircraft, start the engines and taxi to the runway to take off.

The Command Post would be broadcasting a message on the radio. The crews would copy that message and authenticate and decode it in accordance with special encryption-decryption procedures. That message would tell them whether to take off or not. If they had ever received a "go" code, death or destruction were the only things that would stop them.

Practice alerts were conducted to perfect techniques and to assure that the force could meet the predetermined take-off time parameters.

On October 15, 1962, a reconnaissance flight by a United States U-2 spy aircraft revealed the construction of missile bases in Cuba. Photo interpretation revealed they were intended to support intercontinental missile launches from the Island of Cuba.

That information generated a whole lot of nonroutine activity. There was no immediate explanation to the troops. On Lockbourne Air Force Base all training flights were terminated. Aircraft were refueled and their bomb bays loaded with war time ECM transmitters. The aircraft were preflighted and made ready for start and take off. Then they were placed under guard on the ramp.

My crew happened to be one of the aircrews on alert on October 22nd 1963. That was when President John F. Kennedy initiated a "quarantine" of shipping into Cuba. He also warned Premier Kruschev that any missile attack from Cuba would generate a full retaliatory response against the Soviet Union. We were called into the alert force briefing room and told there would be no more practice alerts. We were literally sitting in the cockpit with our finger on the start button. As with men under pressure everywhere there was a little "gallows" humor for the occasion. One of the other crew members asked my copilot, "Geez! Did you see what the alert force cooks are preparing for supper?" My copilot was a bit gullible. "No! What are they makin'." "They're packin' us inflight lunches." Haw, haw, haw. The copilot got a sour look on his face: "That ain't a damn bit funny."

Meanwhile other aircraft that had been generated, loaded and made ready for war were being flown out of Lockbourne. They went to other airports to sit, ready for take off. This was taking place at SAC bases throughout the United

States. We were dispersing our strike force to make it harder for any aggressor to catch us all on the ground.

The situation remained tense for several days. Crews were rotated on and off home-base alert and sent to and from dispersal airports. My crew happened to be sent to Pittsburg. We and the other crews on duty there were wearing flying suits, carrying .38 caliber pistols staying in the airport motel and eating in the terminal restaurant.

My copilot and I were on our tour of duty one evening manning the telephone in our make-shift command center. Any message to launch the force had to be received and authenticated by two people.

The phone rang. I answered. It was the FBI, the Federal Bureau of Investigation. The agent told me that Jimmy Hoffa would be arriving at Pittsburg at such-and-such time.

Jimmy Hoffa was the controversial head of the Teamster's Union. He had been having problems with the Kennedy administration, specifically with Attorney General Robert Kennedy. With all the publicity over this I flippantly asked, "What do you want us to do? Shoot him?"

The agent chuckled and replied, "No, no, but he usually has an entourage of body guards with him. If they see all you guys walking around the terminal with your side arms it might generate an incident." He further suggested that maybe we could arrange not to have any of our crews in the terminal for, say, an hour or so before his arrival 'til an hour or so after.

That sounded like a good plan. And that's what we did.

An apprehensive few days passed until an agreement was reached. The United States promised not to invade Cuba and the Soviets agreed to remove their missiles.

I don't think I overstate things here when I say that that was the greatest, the most formidable strike force the world has ever seen. The agreement brought about a return to our "normal" standard cold-war posture.

The Gift of Wings

Supersonic Flight

An unwritten law seems to say that once Strategic Air Command got 'hold of a person, they never let go. I don't know of anyone who was able to apply and be approved for an assignment outside of SAC. There might have been some but I never heard of them.

I was ready to move on to something new. A new aircraft was coming into the inventory. Applications were being taken. This Aircraft was the General Dynamics B-58 "Hustler" bomber.

Tacticians and engineers were always trying to outperform whatever threats we anticipated. One mantra was to continually fly higher and faster than the other fella. The B-58 was a move in that direction. It would fly mach 2, that's twice the speed of sound, and at altitudes that were too classified to say. It sounded exciting.

A requirement was that whoever applied had to be rated in the top ten percent of all SAC combat crews. I was there. I applied.

I was on leave, at home in Marquette, Michigan,

F-102 "Delta Dagger"

when my navigator called me from Lockbourne Air Force Base. Orders had come in for me. I had been accepted for the B-58 program.

The B-58 is a wasp-waisted four-jet engine delta-wing aircraft. A few problems in the training program had revealed that the flight characteristics of a delta-wing aircraft are different. Some of the otherwise competent pilots were unable to adapt. Failure in a course of training like that can lead to a pilot's loss of rating. As a way around that problem the B-58 program was preceded by a check-out in the F-102 "Delta Dagger" interceptor, a single engine delta wing fighter also built by General Dynamics. The training base for the F-102 was my old instrument instructing base, Perrin Air Force Base in Texas.

The assignment to Perrin was "TDY," that is a designation for a "Tour of Duty," not a permanent change of station. That way, if things didn't go well, a pilot would return to his previous duty station. The move to delta-wing aircraft would be forgotten.

I checked in at Perrin and began training in the F-102. After ground school and a check out in the aircraft (I had no trouble with the delta wing) I was ready for the second high point of F-102 training: supersonic flight!

The aircraft flight manual rated the F-102 at mach 1.5. That's one and one half times the speed of sound. My instructor briefed me, "Climb to 40,000 feet over the designated supersonic corridor, roll over on your back, full military power and head straight down." He paused, looking at me. I guess he was wondering if this "old bomber pilot" would be queasy about pointing an aircraft straight down with the throttle wide open. Getting no adverse response he added, "You'll probably get 1.1 or 1.5, maybe 1.2 if you've got a clean bird."

"But the manual says 1.5," I argued.

He got a kind of pained expression on his face and replied, "Yeah, I know. That's what the book says but that ain't what's gonna happen."

That bothered me. If the manual says something, that's what it's supposed to be! I preflighted my assigned aircraft. All was well. The crew chief helped me get into the seat and strapped in. The start, taxi, and take off were normal.

Supersonic flight generates a sonic "boom." It's caused because, as an aircraft goes supersonic, faster than sound, that's faster than the air can move. The air breaks away around the aircraft like water breaks away around a stick held in the water beside a speed boat. That air coming back together behind the plane generates that boom. That boom also generates a concussion wave that can break windows, crack foundation walls, do all kinds of damage. Because of these problems supersonic flight is restricted to designated open areas and at altitudes above 20,000 feet. That's where I was going now with those thoughts of being short-changed going 'round in my head.

As I was climbing to 40,000 feet I was thinking

if 40,000 is good maybe if I climb to 45,000 feet
- - - and instead of just full throttle, 100 percent
power, why not light the afterburner?

The afterburner on a jet engine injects
additional fuel just aft of the engine. It increases
fuel consumption considerably but it also gives a
heck of an additional boost in power, in thrust.

I climbed to 45,000 feet. I rolled the aircraft
onto its back, pulled the nose straight down – and
lit the afterburner.

Whoop-dee-do!

That aircraft accelerated to mach 1.5 faster than
I can tell you about it. That impressed me and
I thought, "Ben, what the heck are you doing?"
Before it could go faster and possibly tear itself
apart I pulled the throttle back.

Bang! Bang! Bang! The aircraft engine was
experiencing a compressor stall.

A compressor stall occurs when the forward
speed of the aircraft forces more air into the
engine than the engines rotating blades can
ingest. I eased the throttle forward again until
the stalling stopped. While this was going on I
was also easing the stick back to attain straight
and level flight.

The hair had risen on the back of my neck. Having recovered to straight and level flight with the engine appearing to be operating normally I just sat. I didn't move a muscle other than checking the engine gauges by shifting my eyes. All seemed to be working well.

I completed the mission and returned to Perrin and landed. When I reached operations the instructor asked me how it had gone.

"Fine."

"Did you go supersonic?"

"Oh yeah. I got 'er supersonic."

"How fast did she go?"

"She went right up there."

"1.15? 1.2??"

"Yeah, I got to 1.2"

He's a little suspicious of my answers now and is becoming insistent. "How fast did you go?"

Well, I'd been caught. "I made it to 1.5"

"1.5! How in h—l did you do that?"

I told him, not leaving out a thing.

"Geezus ole @ $ *! You're not supposed to do that!"

"I made 'er to 1.5."

So much for supersonic flight.

General Dynamics B-58
"The Hustler"

The Hustler

In spite of my nontraditional supersonic flight in the F-102 I was sent on for training in the B-58 "Hustler" at Carswell Air Force Base.

The training routine was the same as for any other aircraft. It started with ground schooling on the aircraft systems, mechanical, electrical, hydraulic and fuel systems. There was even a bit on weather – there's always a bit on weather.

With the Hustler though we would be operating at higher altitudes where the weather might be a little different. Then too they taught us about high altitude flight – very high altitude flight.

At an altitude of approximately 63,000 feet – that's about 12 miles straight up - the outside air pressure is so low that if a person were exposed to it their blood would boil. The crew's flight compartment could be pressurized and all would be well as long as the cabin didn't lose pressure. There had to be a way to maintain a suitable pressure on anyone operating at those altitudes especially in an emergency.

The first approach was a "space suit" kind of thing. This wasn't very comfortable for long flights and was restrictive of a crewmember's ability to perform his duties. The solution that was adopted was a self-pressurizing capsule to close around the crewmember. Each capsule had a series of overlapping doors, raised above the crewmember's head normally, but made to close on command to seal the man inside. A small window in one of the doors allowed a person to see. In the event of an emergency, the pilot or other flight crew members would raise their seat handles. Their normal safety belt and shoulder harness would automatically pull them back into the capsule. A couple levers, also automatic, would raise the person's knees. At the same time a padded bar came down on his lower shin. All this folded a person up, pulled them inside the capsule and the sliding doors would close and latch. The capsule would pressurize. The whole operation took place almost instantaneously.

A requirement generated by the capsule system was that each crew member had to be pre-measured. If they were too big or if their legs were too long, if they wouldn't fit, well, there was back to the C-47 or some other aircraft for them.

The pilot's capsule included a flight control stick allowing him to control the aircraft. He also had a button he could push that would reduce the throttles. He could then, according to the plan, descend to a livable altitude. Once there each man could release the clamshell doors and raise them to their stowed position.

In the event it became necessary to bail out at any altitude or airspeed (you might be travelling at twice the speed of sound) the capsule would close as described. Next the ejection trigger would be activated and the whole capsule would be ejected. It would free fall to - I seem to remember it would happen around 30,000 feet. At that altitude a drogue parachute would deploy stabilizing the capsule and positioning it so the crewmember was on his back. Then the main parachute would deploy and the capsule would float down to wherever it chanced to land.

This flying business was beginning to get rather complex.

The normal crew positions in a B-58 had the pilot sitting in front with windows on three sides. The Navigator Bombardier was in the second station surrounded by and operating the radar systems including a 'scope of course and various computer controls. The third station was the Defensive Systems Operator.

The Defensive Systems Operator (DSO) assisted the Pilot in operating the aircraft by reading appropriate check lists. His combat purpose was to monitor external electronic activity and counter any threats. He also operated the tail gun, a 20mm "Gatling" type machine gun installed in the tail.

The pilot was the only one who could see

outside. The navigator and the DSO had two small windows at their stations, high and on each side, but they kept them covered so as not to interfere with seeing their radar scopes etc. Each position, although physically near one another, was isolated. There was, at one time, a crawl space between the positions but it became filled with gear.

The B-58 is a relatively small aircraft with what's referred to as a "Wasp Waist." I'll talk about that wasp waist in a minute. Because the aircraft was so small whenever there were modifications or new equipment was installed space was at a premium. This equipment quickly filled the crawl space – and any other nooks and crannies available.

With all this electronic equipment (transistors were just being invented so most of this was vacuum tubes) there was a lot of heat generated. The cockpit pressurization system allowed us to control our cabin temperature. Exhaust air from the cabin would then be routed over the electronic equipment to keep it cool.

If, during flight, the electronic equipment overheated, the air conditioning system was automatically reversed. It now first cooled the electronics and was then vented to us in the cockpit. I've been on several flights when it felt as if we were living in a Sauna. (For you Non Scandinavians, a sauna is a Finnish Steam Bath.)

We, the crew, could report these heating/ cooling problems when we landed. What was happening, so the scuttlebutt had it, was that the electronics people claimed the air conditioning wasn't keeping their equipment cool. The air conditioning people, on the other hand, claimed their system was working "in accordance with specifications" and that the electronics was not working as advertised. These new transistors were coming into use to miniaturize our equipment and I personally believe these and our lack of knowledge about them was the culprit.

Many are the flights when I've heard the navigator moaning and wailing about his equipment doing things not in the manuals. If it happened to be when we were on a practice bombing run, I would look outside the cockpit and, when I felt lucky, sing out, "Let 'er go!" Sometimes I "hit" the target as well as all that super radar equipment could.

Lemme get the "Wasp Waist" explanation in here and then we'll move on to something else.

When General Dynamic was first designing supersonic aircraft – the F-102 was the first, I believe. They were running wind-tunnel tests of the design but couldn't get it up to supersonic speed. The problem was a sort of "air-bubble" that would form along the aircraft fuselage creating more drag and preventing supersonic speed. The engineers were trying one thing and another and tearing their hair out. Then, so the story I was told, a junior grade engineer said, "Why not squeeze the fuselage, make a space for that bubble?" They tried it. It worked. So the "Wasp Waist" came to be. I never heard what happened to that "Wasp Waist" engineer. Maybe he wound up running the company?

If there's a choice between a specialist with education and a specialist with imagination, go with the imagination. Of course if you've got both . . .

B-58 "Hustler" - night takeoff

60,000 pounds of thrust

from those engines.

A Homesick Angel

Flight in a B-58 was a whole new experience. After checking out all the systems, lining up on the runway, you reach over and push the four throttles forward. At 100% military power, raise the throttles slightly and push forward another inch or so into the afterburner range. Power output leaps from 40,000 pounds of thrust military power, to something over 60,000 pounds of thrust with afterburners - instantaneously. That'll put a person back into their seat.

On all jet aircraft the take-off ground roll is pre-computed. A recognizable point on the runway is selected at which, depending on the airspeed attained, a decision made to continue taking off or to throttle back and abort. In the past several jet aircraft have run off the far end of the runway never having attained flying speed. This intermediate airspeed check point, "S-1" it's called, determines whether or not the aircraft is accelerating "on schedule." I can remember the days when a pilot pushed the throttles forward whenever he felt lucky. The take-off checks are a really good thing.

Once airborne, even with a fully grossed out aircraft (163,000 pounds) the nose comes up and up just maintaining climb speed.

The airport is just on the edge of Fort Worth. When taking off to the south aircraft passed over a populated section of the city. At a highway intersection a mile or so off the end of the runway was a motel. A number of the troops coming to Carswell for training would stay there while they searched for a house in the area. Sometimes, if we knew who was staying at the motel and if it was an early morning take off, we'd hold 'er down to a hundred feet or so and go over the motel with the afterburners roaring. It was intended as a sort of wake-up call. We probably woke up everybody on that end of town.

In flight the aircraft handled as gently as a baby carriage. This wasn't an easy task to accomplish – for the aircraft engineers that is. The B-58 was eighty tons of aircraft traveling at speeds up to over 1,300 miles per hour. This was the fastest aircraft in the world in its day. To gain a feel for this speed, 1,300 miles per hour is about 22 miles per minute, 1,900 feet per second. A 30-30 rifle muzzle velocity, depending on the cartridge, ranges from 1,600 to 2,600 feet per second. B-58 aircrews have travelled "faster than a speeding bullet" and, of course, "topped tall buildings at a single bound." How about that?

Airflow, especially in what's called the transonic range: when airflow over some surfaces of the aircraft reached the speed of sound until the whole aircraft was traveling supersonic, created shock waves and varying pressures and responses from the flight control surfaces. This could complicate aircraft control but all this test-program data was entered into a computer system. The flight controls are actually moved by hydraulic pistons. The movement is initiated by the pilot. The computer program gives varying control movements to get the desired effect without overstressing of the airframe. The program also provides artificial "feel" to the pilot's flight controls giving him the sensations of flight.

When traversing from subsonic flight to supersonic flight and back, what's called "the center of pressure" moves over a considerable range. The center of pressure is where the lift forces of the aircraft are centered.

If you balance a pencil on your finger, the point where it balances is the "center of pressure." Suppose you move your finger. The pencil no longer balances – unless you move a weight of some kind to the "light" end of the pencil. That's what the crew does in the B-58, they rapidly transfer fuel from front to rear – or the reverse. It can get a little tricky.

What about in-flight problems? A person must always be prepared for this. There are warning lights but a crewmember is often pretty busy with other things. To overcome this problem there is a tape recording that will come onto the intercom to warn of what's gone – or going – wrong. Picture this: you're supersonic in the middle of a bomb run coming up on the bomb release point. A fighter aircraft is closing in, attempting to intercept you. The three crew members are talking on the intercom, coordinating their responses. Suddenly a sultry female voice interrupts with, "Your number four engine is about to explode." That'll get your attention! That's another system of the B-58.

Supersonic flight over the United States are restricted to certain more unpopulated areas and restricted to altitudes above 20,000 feet. The reason for this is the "sonic boom" supersonic flight creates. When any object is travelling at supersonic speed, the air is unable to get out of the way smoothly. A shock wave, high pressure forms in front of the object. Air pressure decreases along the length of the object until, after it has passed, "normal" air pressure claps together behind it. On the ground this creates concussion, a "boom." It creates, in fact, a double boom – one from the front compression wave and the second, almost immediate, from the rear. The reason for the altitude limit is that the concussion waves have the capability of breaking windows, cracking foundation walls and other such damage.

The profile of a supersonic training flight – I'm reaching back in memory for this – is to climb above 20,000 feet, open the throttles, light the afterburners and accelerate to 400 miles per hour "indicated." The airspeed indicator would show 400 mph but the aircraft, because of the high altitude and thin air, would actually be moving at over 500 mph. We would then climb, holding the airspeed at 400 indicated until we intercepted Mach 2, twice the speed of sound. We would continue climbing at mach 2 until we reached whatever altitude we desired – up to the aircraft service ceiling of 63,000 feet, twelve miles up.

While flying this profile one day we were still in level flight around 24,000 feet. When I hadn't yet started to climb the air traffic controller became concerned. There was a B-52 jet bomber coming the other way, level and much slower. That B-52 and I passed one another. He was heading east at about 300mph while I was heading west at about 700 mph. I saw him. I don't know whether he saw us or not. Either way we passed at something like 1,000 miles per hour, too fast to wave.

While flying this supersonic profile this is what's happening; shock waves are forming and moving over the aircraft. A point is reached (remember the bang bang bang in the F-102?) where the engines cannot ingest as much air as is being forced in on them. As this point approaches, the center cone in each engine intake begins to move forward closing down the opening. It restricts inlet air to what the engine can handle.

It's all done automatically.

As the aircraft goes supersonic, I, in the front cockpit can look out my window and see that supersonic shock wave that forms ahead of each of the inboard engines. If you've ever looked through an old – or cheap – pane of glass and seen the distortion, that ripple where the glass varies in thickness, that's what that shock wave looks like – a distortion while looking through the air.

The Gift of Wings

The Fly-By

The flight control system and a few other systems are operated by hydraulics. As a safety feature the system is redundant – there are two hydraulic systems doing the same thing. If during flight one of these systems should fail or malfunction the rule is to get the plane on the ground as soon as you can. If that second system should fail also, well, you have just become nothing but a passenger.

Strategic Air Command was a very autocratic command. Everything was controlled from SAC headquarters in Omaha, Nebraska: "Our father who art in Omaha" – that sort of thing.

To keep a finger on the pulse of the force periodic no-notice Operational Readiness Inspections (ORIs) inspections would be conducted. The inspectors would literally sneak onto the base – maybe land at a nearby civilian airport and drive to the base, for example. The whole purpose was to give no warning at all that they were coming.

When they hit the base, some would go to the command post, some to the maintenance facility, to the key control spots. Folks working in these sections would be kept from warning or alerting anyone. Then they'd wait for an alert message to scramble the force they already knew would be coming from Omaha. They were trying to simulate what would happen if a war started.

The crews on alert would first learn what was happening when the klaxon sounded sending them rushing to their aircraft. They would start engines as they received the (practice) message, taxi to the runway, open the throttles as if to take off, start to roll down the runway but then pull the power back and taxi back to the ramp. The flight crews would then go back to the alert barracks where they would be subject to written examinations pertaining to the war plan, the mission and their part in it.

Meanwhile maintenance crews would be downloading non-alert aircraft of their training gear and uploading wartime loads. Unlike actual war they weren't loading nor would we be carrying any nuclear weapons.

The alert aircraft could have no maintenance

performed other than download of the weapons. The crews would be flying those aircraft on a simulated wartime mission including on-time take off, in-flight refueling, navigation and a simulated bomb run. All this would be watched closely in determining a score for the whole Bomb Wing. A failing score could shake up the careers and assignments for the wing staff members. This was serious stuff.

Everything was tested. There were even physical fitness tests, sit ups, push ups, a whole range of exercises. And it was all scored. A Wing that failed an inspection could have dire consequences for the commander.

One of the crews, while in flight during an ORI, experienced a failure of one of the hydraulic systems. By the book they immediately aborted their mission and landed at the nearest installation; Ellsworth Air Force Base near Rapid City, South Dakota.

The crew left the airplane and returned home. The rest of the inspection continued. Later maintenance sent a ground crew to Ellsworth to repair the aircraft. Still later, after the aircraft was reported as repaired and airworthy, operations were casting about for a crew to go to Ellsworth and fly the aircraft back. I was always ready to fly anywhere at any time. There were a couple of "Wing Weenies" (a flight crew's pet name for the higher ups) who wanted to get a little flying time also. We made up the crew.

When we arrived at Ellsworth I knew the crew chief on the repair crew quite well. The ground crews are pretty savvy about the flight crews. They know who's going to be hard to handle and who the more understanding individuals are. I always believed, maybe it's conceit but, having come up through the ranks, from Staff Sergeant to the officer ranks, I believed the crew chief felt freer to be more open with me. A guy who has come up though the ranks is called "a mustang." Anyway I always felt I had a closer relationship with the ground crews than many of the other flight crews did.

So, this crew chief was someone I felt I knew pretty well. Evidently he did too. When he saw me he put out his hand and said, "Major! Am I ever glad to see you."

The B-58 on the ground is a rather spindly looking thing. In the air, with her wheels tucked under her skirt, she's a thing of beauty. If she could have cooked, I would have married one.

Ellsworth was a B-52 base – big heavy bombers - with the emphasis on the heavy. The crew chief told me that, in the Non Commissioned Officer's (NCO) Club, he and his crew had been taking a bit of good natured razzing about their crippled bird. "Geez, Major, could you give us a fly-by on the way out?" Do bears poop in the woods? I told him I'd see what I could do.

It was a weekend, a Sunday when we were to fly the airplane back home. After we had checked the weather, planned the trip and filed our flight plan and just before going out to the aircraft, I called the control tower on the telephone. "Say, I'm here to pick up the B-58 and I'd like to check on the directional equipment. Could I possibly fly down the runway after take off?"

There was a brief pause, then - I could almost see the grin on the guys face – "Yeah! Sure! You bet you can. Call when you turn inbound to be sure there's no other traffic."

"Thanks." I was grinning too.

When we got to the aircraft and, after a cursory preflight and strapping into my seat, I gave the chief a "thumbs up" so he'd know it was in the works.

We taxied out, lined up and took off. The aircraft wasn't fully loaded for the short flight home so she was eager as a young colt. Once in the air I told the crew what we were about to do. The airplane was accelerating smartly and I held it low and level. I turned ninety degrees to the right and then two hundred seventy degrees to the left, turning around in a manner so as to be lined up with the runway. Just to be sure, I had tuned in Ellsworth's instrument landing system. A vertical needle on the instrument panel would confirm that I was aligned properly.

With the airplane moving as fast as it was, it was taking a while to get it turned around. As I turned inbound I called the control tower operator. There was no conflicting traffic and he told me to "bring 'er on in."

In the meantime the crew chief had told the ground crew that I would make a fly-by. They had stood around the crew stand on the ramp watching and waiting. As time passed some of them grew impatient.

"Aww, he ain't comin'"

"Yes, he is. He told me he would. He'll be here." Some of the guys headed back toward base operations.

I was inbound, going fast and still accelerating. A quick glance at the airspeed indicator showed over 600 mph and increasing. That was coming pretty close to supersonic speed, about 700.

I told you about the computer controlled flight control system. At the speed I was travelling it was beginning to restrict my control movements. I was going to have to be careful here. We leveled out just over the runway – low over the runway. About midway down the field I pulled the nose straight up and lit the four afterburners. There must have been a heck of a BOOM on the ground. We went from ground level to 35,000 feet, about seven miles up in less time than it takes to tell you about it. From there on the flight was normal normal. The autopilot flew the airplane. The navigator navigated and the systems operator operated his systems. I just stayed awake.

Later, back at the home station, the crew chief looked me up. "I wanna thank you, Major." Those who had walked back to operations said the whole control tower shook when we passed. The crew chief continued, "Me and my crew went to the NCO club that night, got drunk on our butts and couldn't pay for a thing."

That's what life's all about.

"Boom!"

All aircraft develop problems. The Federal Aviation Administration and Air Force Safety Programs try to keep track of any and all problems, even the little ones. The reason is that they assemble these reports to see if they predict developing trouble areas or trends. With newer model aircraft the scrutiny is even more important.

When the B-58 was designed it was the fastest aircraft in the air. The systems and technology that created her were right at the fingertips of the state of the art.

In an attempt to gain information each aircraft take-off was filmed. At a total gross weight of 163,000 pounds and approximately 90,000 pounds of that being fuel, any take off accidents other than minor incidents tended to end in total demolition of the aircraft by fire.

An incident occurred during a take off (by another crew, not me) in which there was an explosion just after leaving the ground. The aircraft was momentarily out of control but the pilot was able to regain control and managed to keep it in the air. He was able to circle the field and land. The crewmember in the third station, the systems operator, was killed.

The film of the take off plus examination of the aircraft after landing revealed that the starter on the number two engine had disintegrated.

The engine starters were pneumatic, driven by compressed air. Ground crew would plug about a four inch diameter hose into the aircraft. The pilot would activate the starter which would automatically engage the engine and accelerate until it had the engine turning at 8% or so of its maximum RPM. At that point the pilot would activate the ignition and the jet exhaust gasses would further accelerate the engine speed. The starter would disengage and the procedure would be repeated on the next engine.

It was determined, from the film of the take off and the subsequent examination that the starter on the number two engine had failed to disengage. Instead of it turning the engine, the engine was now turning the starter. At take off power settings that small impellor was spinning at ten times its design speed. It disintegrated sending hot metal fragments into the aircraft's under slung fuel tank which caused the explosion of that fuel while other bits of this shrapnel tore through the aircraft fuselage killing the systems operator.

Modifications were made to the starter and the starting procedure. Ground crewmen were ever after this required to check after engine start that the starter had disengaged.

The Air Force had purchased 116 B-58 aircraft of which 26 were lost to accidents. Aircraft systems failure caused several of these losses. When an accident occurs at high altitude and during supersonic flight the odds of crewmembers survival are not good.

These losses are the cost paid for progress and underline the fact that freedom is not free.

The Gift of Wings

Photo Reconnaissance

The B-58 had also been considered as a reconnaissance aircraft. During the Cuban missile crisis in 1962 a B-58 equipped with a camera overflew Cuba.

In 1963 several B-58 aircraft were outfitted to be reconnaissance aircraft. The modification involved installing a camera capable of photographing "from horizon to horizon" (left and right) in the pod carried under the aircraft. Controls were installed in the Navigator Bombardier station.

The reason for this new mission capability, so we were told, was the development of surface to air missiles by China. Up to then reconnaissance was being conducted by RF-101 "Voodoo" twin engine jet fighter aircraft. They accomplished their mission by over-flight at high altitude. Surface to air missiles posed an unacceptable threat to that operation.

It was decided to counter the missile threat by conducting future reconnaissance at low altitude and high speed. The RF-101 was fast but carried a limited amount of fuel. The B-58 was better suited to this new mission requirement. As it turned out, neither aircraft flew any of those missions. Other than the over-flight of Cuba the B-58 capability was used for rapid photography of natural disasters such as the Earthquake in Alaska in March, 1964.

Training flights for the reconnaissance mission, especially those at low altitude, were always an interesting and often exciting thing. One of our practice targets was a grain silo in a remote area of West Texas. The land was pretty flat and finding that silo sticking up was not a difficult problem.

On one of the flights the crew came back with a close up of a little shack constructed atop the silo. Not to be outdone the next crew to fly that mission brought back not only a picture of the shack but a readable photo of the "No Trespassing" notice posted on the shack door.

Another interesting photo taken along that same route was of a cowboy and a herd of cattle. Keep in mind now that the B-58, even when subsonic at low altitude, was flying pretty much ahead of the noise it made. Interpreting this photo we assumed the cowboy hadn't heard the aircraft approaching until the last second or two – maybe he happened to look up and see it approaching. The photo frame was filled with a startled horse and the cowboy half-way dismounted in an attempt to duck we surmised. As I said, we were flying at low altitude.

When word of some of these more spectacular shots made its way up the chain of command, a directive came back down. We were given a minimum altitude we were to fly. There would be no exceptions – or else.

Aah, your tax dollars at work.

" An autobiography usually reveals

nothing bad about the writer

- Except his memory."

Franklin P. Jones

You are Selected

This next has nothing to do with airplanes and you may want to skip it. Since all this I'm writing is a sort of "career path" I wouldn't want any youngsters who might read it to assume it was all fun and games. There was a lot of "grunt" work involved. That's a little of what's next. Suit yourself if you want to bother with it or not.

It was in 1966 that I was notified that I had been selected to attend Air Command and Staff College at Maxwell Air Force Base at Montgomery, Alabama. Whoop-dee-doo!

There's a promotion path, a sequence, a series of steps that a professional soldier pretty much must follow to rise in rank. In the officer ranks it's a series of continuous training steps. The first is attaining a commission, starting out as a second lieutenant. The military academies, West Point, Annapolis, the Air Force Academy are thought of as the true professional's starting point but a number of those attending them will receive an education, serve a minimum time in uniform and seek a career elsewhere.

Others gain a commission through college ROTC (Reserve Officer Training Corp) and some of us through service conducted commissioning schools. The academy graduates enter service as Regular Officers. The rest of us put on our commission as Reserve Officers. The reserve officers are looked upon as filling in the ebb and flow of the service requirements. When there's a war, call in the reserves. When there's no war, the core military are the regulars. There are exceptions but, basically, that's the way it was planned.

Starting out, an ambitious young Air Force officer tries to attend Squadron Officers School. If he is not able to go for whatever reason he has the opportunity to take the courses by correspondence.

Assuming he gets this far, a board of some sort meets annually to review the records of all officers who meet their requirements. This board will select who will attend Air Command and Staff School. This is not a school such as Squadron Officers School that an officer may apply to attend. Air Command and Staff is by selection and readies Officers for field grade, Major, Lieutenant Colonel and Colonel assignments. The next up the ladder is the General Officers Course.

I was a reserve officer. I didn't have a college degree although I was steadily taking correspondence courses (that's how I completed Squadron Officer's School) and attending college classes nights. I was simply a high school graduate – and hadn't done that well in high school. As soon as I was commissioned a Second Lieutenant I became aware that the fellas on either side of me had college training. There was no overt discrimination here it was just me looking around and realizing who I would be competing against.

When I was first notified that I had been selected I was a little upset. My immediate thought was that someone had stepped on my computer punch card (that's what computers used in those days) with their golf shoes and my selection would be discovered to be a mistake. If you're not selected for something, what the heck, you're still one of the boys. If you are selected and then rejected, there's a sort of stigma attached. That's what I feared would happen.

It didn't. I went to Alabama.

Let me digress here to talk about something I learned in General Curtis LeMay's Strategic Air Command. There are always regulations to guide a person in what they should do. There are Flying Safety rules and regulations too. If you think about it, the safest approach to flying is to never leave the ground. We all operate in between there somewhere.

When flying training missions you're sent out to accomplish "A," "B," "C," and so on. When you land you're debriefed on the mission. "Did you accomplish 'A,' 'B,' 'C,' and so on?" "Well, there was this and that and "snow capped mountains and shark infested waters" but we did manage to . ." Everyone nods sagely and sympathetically.

Another crew comes in to be debriefed. "Did you accomplish 'A,' 'B,' 'C,' and so on?" "Yes, sir."

When promotions come around, guess who gets promoted?

I entered the Air Command and Staff course like a country boy on his first trip to the city. What was I doing here? After a few days I recalled something President Harry Truman said back when he was first elected to Congress. He first wondered how a dumb fella like him had ever been elected to the Congress of the United States. Then he wondered how so many of those other dumb so-and-so's had ever gotten elected.

Now we come to the "coulda – woulda – shoulda" excuses. Those graduates scoring in the top ten percent of the class, if they weren't already regular officers, would be offered a regular officers commission. I wasn't offered one. I shoulda worked harder. Ah, well, as my wife, Dorothy, says, "Don't be looking back. It's a waste of time."

Anyone assigned to Strategic Air Command had an extensive background check conducted on them. The word was once SAC got hold of you, write your mother and tell her to sell the outhouse. Your butt belongs to SAC.

The Viet Nam War was going strong when we graduated from Air Command and Staff. The Air Force was rotating personnel. A tour in 'Nam was one year and back home. They needed pilots in the pipeline and I was a pilot. I was sent to

George Air Force Base in California to train in the F-4 "Phantom" fighter bomber.

A new adventure was coming up.

If you younger fellas read this, the point I'm trying to make is that education and hard work are important. Work at it and learn even if you don't immediately know why or where you'll need what's being taught.

I was raised on a farm. You've got to spade the dirt, handle a little manure now and then if you want to succeed. The Golden Rule says "Do unto others as you would have them do unto you." The "promotion" version of that rule says, "Promote the guy or gal who can get the job done."

McDonnel Douglas F-4 Fighter Bomber

The Phantom

Sunny California sounded like a pretty nice place to be. It was. George Air Force Base is by Apple Valley on the plateau above San Bernadino. Roy Rogers and Dale Evans were my neighbors in Apple Valley. They had a beautiful ranch home there. I stayed in a motel next door for a couple days.

The F-4s at George Air Force Base were rugged high performance aircraft. A first impression was that it wasn't exactly beautiful. More likely it would be called ugly, but it was mean ugly. Not to those of us who flew it but to anyone who went up against it.

Fighter pilots are a unique bunch. There's a saying: "You can always tell a fighter pilot – but you can't tell him much."

The people are selected for a course of training. They may be selected because of their aptitude or how they score on a written examination or maybe by some psychological evaluation. There is an overriding consideration - what the military has need of at the time.

That was how I happened to get in the flying business. The Air Force demanded college education until the Korean War generated an increased demand. They reduced the requirements to "see light and hear thunder." That's when I stepped forward.

Throughout a person's flight training they would be evaluated, among other attributes, on their aggressiveness. A fighter pilot should be aggressive. Attack!

The centralized control I had been used to in SAC was not what I encountered in Tactical Air Command (TAC). My personal opinion is that TAC could have used a bit of that centralized control but that's just my thought.

I was a little slow at figuring out what the capabilities of the F-4 as a weapon system were and how I could best utilize them. Then I set to work trying to maximize my ability to make them work.

This may sound a bit conceited and it probably is. I believe though that if you intend to fly fighter aircraft you'd better believe you're the best aviator to hold a stick and throttle. If you go into the fight believing that other guy is better - he probably will be.

First was the ground school on the aircraft, its systems and some of the techniques for getting the most out of it. Then came the basic check out, how to take off and land. Then you were introduced to basic maneuvers. After that it was a matter of practice.

An F-4 crew is composed of the pilot or aircraft commander in the front cockpit. The weapon system operator rode in the rear cockpit. Sometimes the rear seat crewmember would be a rated Navigator rather than a pilot. All this terminology was quickly simplified. There's the "Guy in Back," the GIB, and the "Guy in Front," the GIF. It worked.

The pilot, the GIB I crewed with was a freshly graduated pilot but a fine young fella. There was one small incident wherein I hope I steered him in the right direction.

I mentioned that I had been a Staff Sergeant prior to breaking into the commissioned ranks. I guess that's why I have always had a feel for the troops in the ranks.

Anyway, we had been scheduled to fly, walked

out to the aircraft and found that some routine ground crew preparation hadn't been finished. My young GIB proceeded to chew out the crew chief. I waited until he had finished then the two of us started walking back to operations.

I waited until we were far enough away that the GIB wouldn't feel I was embarrassing him in front of the ground crew. It was, however, not so far that the ground crewmen wouldn't recognize that the GIB was getting a little instruction of his own. I talked about being ground crew, some of their problems and how a little understanding could often pay big dividends.

A little later but before we completed our training the lad had a chance to transfer to a single engine single pilot training program, a promotion of sorts. I gave him my best recommendation and wished him well.

My next GIB was a very sharp and competent young fella. I would learn to appreciate him more and more as time passed.

It was assumed by all that we would be sent to Viet Nam upon completion of training. It came as a surprise that I was sent to Eglin Air Force Base in the panhandle of Florida instead.

Eglin by the Sea

On the way to Eglin Air Force Base in Florida I stopped "Home" (Home. To me has always been Michigan's Upper Peninsula). My mother and father had purchased an Avion travel trailer and had travelled with it touring the country. After my father's death the trailer had been parked. I borrowed the trailer from my mother and took it to sunny Florida.

When leaving Northern Michigan – it was winter – I came on a long snow covered hill just east of Munising. I couldn't get up that hill. The wheels were just spinning. A county grader came along pushing back the snow on the shoulder of the road. We were both going in the same direction. I was literally spinning my wheels and was in his way. He cheerfully attached a chain to my rig, continued to grade the side of the road and pulled me up the hill. There are a lot of good folks around.

I was able to rent a parking slip right on the water at Fort Walton Beach near the Air Base and checked in. I was assigned to a squadron that had the latest model F-4's – the "E" model – with a built-in 20 mm Gatling gun. This was going to be fun.

The planners of wars had determined that air-to-air combat would henceforth be fought with missiles, ground to air, air to air and the days of the old fashioned aerial dog fighting were done. The guys in Viet Nam quickly told them that this was not so.

The two missiles we were equipped with were the "Sidewinder" heat seeking air-to-air missile and the "Sparrow," a radar homing air-to-air missile.

Both missiles had to be fired at a given range from the target to allow the missile engine to ignite, accelerate, arm itself (we didn't want any missiles to detonate right under our aircraft) and guide itself to the target.

When the sidewinder had acquired a target the noise in the pilots headphones went from a low amplitude buzzing, like frying bacon, to a vicious snarling sound. That's when you could fire it.

The Sparrow missile was a bit more complex. The systems operator in the F-4 had to "acquire" the target on the radar and lock on so the radar would track the target. The Sparrow missile would receive that same radar return signal and, when fired, would follow it to the target. The complication was that you had to continue radar tracking which meant following whatever aircraft you were firing at. If that target aircraft had a buddy around he wouldn't be too happy about that situation and he had a gun!

There were other problems. The sidewinder might decide to try to hit the sun instead of the target. If the target released flares it might go after a flare. The Sparrow might get a return signal from the ground and head for the ground.

Then, too, there was always the possibility of a malfunction. One of the guys fired a missile that just fell, tumbled, then ignited and shot up past the cockpit. It was so close "I could have lit a cigarette," the pilot said. It's kind of embarrassing if you shoot yourself down.

Machine guns, although a complex mechanism, are not so temperamental. The problem in air-to-air gunnery is the time the fighter has to fire.

During World War I aircraft moved a lot slower and a single machine gun firing, "put-put-put,"

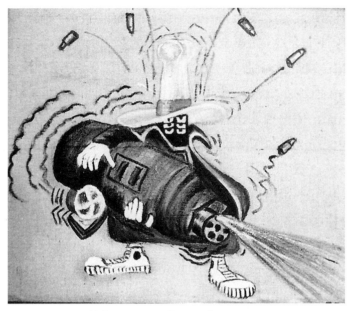

Phantom 2 gatling gun

was often enough to do the job. A problem with firing the gun through the propeller was that the pilot would often shoot off his own propeller. It was a German engineer who developed a fix for the problem. He built a mechanical connection between the engine and the machine gun that synchronized the firing to times the propeller was cross-ways.

During World War II aircraft were moving much faster. We mounted several guns along the wings or in the nose. All would fire at once.

With the coming of jet aircraft, speeds increased

even more. With the speed and maneuverability of the aircraft, the time the guns were aligned with the target and ready to fire was greatly reduced. You had to get a lot of fire power out in just a couple seconds. That brought on the Gatling gun. It had been developed for the American Civil War but saw limited use. When fitted to aircraft, it had several barrels which reduced the possibility of melting the gun barrel. The barrels were mounted around a central tubing. The whole thing rotated allowing the various barrels to be loaded, fired, shell casings ejected and reloaded repeatedly. The gun on the F-4E could fire (bear with me here – I'm reaching a long way back) up to 600 rounds per minute – that's ten rounds per second. A regular fire hose. We only carried about 700 rounds so no one just fired and held down the trigger.

Firing at ground targets the firing pattern was set at a fixed range and the aircraft was travelling about 400 mph. The time the aircraft was at the proper range for a hit was extremely short. I used to just hit the trigger and release it as quickly as I could. The shortest burst I ever got off was 47 rounds – and they all hit the target (I'm bragging a bit here but, what the heck, I was a fighter pilot).

Once again – and I almost feel like a traitor here – Tactical Air Command was a rather loose hung outfit. A training flight would go out to the firing range, fire rockets, drop (practice) bombs and fire guns at a ground target. When we landed no one was there to ask "Did you accomplish 'A,' 'B,' etc." The runs were scored and we eagerly got our scores. After that we'd all go over to the officer's club and have a drink.

Living in my little travel trailer I began drawing diagrams and figuring trajectories and firing ranges and applying what I had figured out to what I was trying to do in the air. I got pretty darned good – and the powers that be noticed – and it came back to bite me in the you know where.

Highjacked!

Those high scores I was getting on the bombing and gunnery range brought me to the attention of a particular Squadron Commander. This commander had been charged with assembling a newly developing "weapon of war." He pointed his finger, by way of the Wing Commander, and said, "I want you!"

This new unit, the 25th TAC Fighter Squadron, was still flying the older model F-4Ds. I was anxious to stay in the E model, the one with the gun. I wiggled and squirmed and tried to get out of it but all to no avail. I reported in to the 25th TAC Fighter Squadron, ready for duty.

The 25th had been selected to perfect a technique for placing sensors along the Ho Chi Minh trail. The Ho Chi Minh trail was a network of dirt roadways, foot paths and burro trails that carried supplies from North Viet Nam to various Viet Cong positions in South Viet Nam. The necessary method of delivery wasn't consistent with what TAC pilots were accustomed to. These were rather sensitive electronic devices. There were two basic types: a seismic sensor and an audio sensor.

The seismic sensor looked like a huge nail, about two or two and one half feet in diameter, and six or seven feet long. It was pointed on one end (to penetrate into the earth) with a broad flat "nail head" on the other end, much like the head of a spike. Coming out of that nail head was a three foot or so pale green flexible plastic sort of tree branch thing. The idea was to drop this device so that it drove into the ground. The "nail head" prevented it from going completely out of sight. The "tree branch" was an inconspicuous transmitting antenna. Passing trucks, troops, whatever would generate seismic vibrations which the device would detect. A battery operated transmitter would turn on and transmit these vibration signals to a C-130 transport plane, a relay station, circling overhead. The C-130 would in turn relay these signals to a battery of computers which would locate the device by its frequency. It would analyze the vibrations and tell the intelligence people that at that very moment, there were – whatever it decided made the vibrations – moving past that sensor. It sounded like a good idea.

The audio sensors were about the same size but lacked the pointed end and the nail head. These were dropped by parachute so as to hang in trees. They would detect any audible sounds and respond just like the seismic devices.

A major problem was placing these devices in exact locations. If we didn't know where the device was located, it could send all sorts of signals but we wouldn't know where they were. Nowadays, with global positioning devices, these sensors could probably transmit their precise locations.

The troops in the 25th TAC Fighter Squadron were accustomed to diving down from altitude and flinging bombs and firing rockets and shooting guns. This new mission was like asking a bunch of lumberjacks to serve an afternoon tea. We were having problems.

I guess my experience with SAC, dropping nuclear bombs from level flight at low altitudes, gave me a better insight to what we were trying to do.

Also, that lad, Denny Lipp, I had riding in the

rear seat was nothing but a sharp troop. As I go through these stories saying "I," in so far as the airplane and the mission is concerned, you might want to read it as "we." It wouldn't be too many months before that lad would be responsible for brushing the angel of death off my shoulders more than once.

The squadron was still in the middle of developing techniques and procedures for dropping these devices when the fat hit the fan. It was 1968. The North Vietnamese and the Viet Cong launched what came to be called the TET offensive. One of the questions that was asked was how did they get all those arms and equipment to South Viet Nam without us knowing?

I don't think the smoke over Hue or Saigon had cleared before we had orders to deploy to Southeast Asia. We departed Eglin as a complete squadron, lock, stock and barrel. Those of us who flew the aircraft took off early one morning and headed west. We joined a flight of KC-135 aerial tanker aircraft over Texas. Together we proceeded west, refueling in flight as necessary, and landed in Hawaii. The next day we flew on to Midway Island. The day after that we took

F-4s and KC-135 Tanker Aircraft

off and headed west again. Over the Philippine Islands we topped off again from our tankers. The tankers landed at Clark Air Force Base in the Phillippines and we continued to Southeast Asia. Our destination was Ubon Royal Thai Air Force Base at Ubon, Thailand.

We would be stationed in Thailand because our mission involved North Viet Nam and Laos with very little in-country Viet Nam activity.

The F-4 had electronic warfare monitoring equipment. Down in the lower right corner of the pilot's instrument panel was a small oscilloscope, maybe three inches in diameter. There was also an audio detection device which, when the pilot listened to it, would give him the familiar (to pilots) "weep - - weep - - weep" of scanning radar. It also picked up the snarling sound of missile guidance signals being sent to a SAM (Surface to Air Missile).

While we were peacefully flying over South Viet Nam enroute to Thailand that sudden snarl broke the silence. A strobe on the radar detector pointed off to the two o'clock position. This wasn't supposed to happen? There was silence for the space of twenty seconds or so. Then someone said, "Did you guys hear that?" "Yeah." "That's a SAM signal ain't it?" "Yeah."

Again there was silence for twenty or thirty seconds. Then someone said, "I guess he missed?"

As we approached Ubon we came under attack – a mock attack – by the Australian Air Force.

The Aussies had a squadron of F-86s stationed at Ubon. This was a show of support from Australia, a member of SEATO (South East Asia Treaty Organization). The Aussies, however, were prohibited from engaging the enemy unless the enemy attacked Ubon. They weren't allowed to get into the fight and they were burning up with frustration. They attacked us in mock combat and we, in our heavily loaded F-4s, twisted and turned with them but without much success.

One F-86 driver came at us and I managed to get behind him – bad news for him. He began a "scissors" maneuver, rapid and hard turns left and right, designed to make the aircraft behind overshoot. I followed him, honking that poor old F-4 so hard we pretty near fell out of the sky – but we never did overshoot him. Score one for us!

The troops at Ubon were anticipating our arrival. They met us with crew vans, trucks, bicycles whatever they had. The contingent from Eglin who had flown over in transports arrived also and we partied for the rest of the day and on into the night.

The next day, things got serious.

"War hath no fury like a

non-combatant."

C.E. Montague

Over 200 bombs in one drop;
51 tons of explosives

Southeast Asia

The first order of business was several days of ground school. This war was extremely political in nature and there were rules we had to abide by. It always seems that it's people not involved in the actual fighting who make all these rules. Some of the lectures had to do with the threats we would face, what had been learned about our opponents thus far, search and rescue procedures, airborne command and control, useful things like that.

After this preparation we were scheduled as wing men on missions with an experienced back-seater to help us along. I can remember first time I rolled in on an attack and the fellas on the ground started shooting.

Depending upon how the feed for the weapon is set, there's usually a tracer bullet every five or six rounds fired. One of the rules concerning tracers is that they work both ways. It shows the gunner where his rounds are going so he can adjust his aim. It also shows whoever he's shooting at where the rounds are coming from so there can be an adjustment there also.

Looking down at those tracers coming up and remembering that there are five or six times that many rounds heading your way makes an impression. The words of my father concerning a childhood fight came to mind: "Don't you run!" Well, dad, for whatever it's worth now, I didn't run.

One of the experienced back-seaters I flew with was the guy who'd been my navigator bombardier back in the B-47s. He was still a navigator but had been one of those chosen to see how a navigator would work out in the second seat. We had a reunion but it was rather short. I had just got there and he was about to return to the 'states.

After a few missions we were deemed qualified. We knew the rules and could find our way back to the home station. Now we turned to the sensor mission, named by the powers that be "Igloo White."

We were still developing delivery techniques. Most of what we had been trying back in the 'states hadn't been working that well. We were going to have to learn more on the job.

Combat Crew In Action

Put the word on Uncle Ho

Sensors to be loaded on our aircraft would be selected by evaluating the reconnaissance photos of where they were supposed to go. I say "supposed to go" because there were times they didn't get there.

It was important to this whole concept of eavesdropping that two requisites be satisfied: the units had to be placed close to the specified segment of the trail they were to monitor and once they were delivered, we had to know precisely where they had landed.

To help with this second part our aircraft carried cameras that took a series of photos as we were releasing the units. Upon landing the film would be taken from the camera developed, printed and given to photo interpreters. These photo interpreters would attempt to match our photos to photos of the selected target area. There was a signal on our photos indicating when the release had occurred. Then, utilizing information supplied by the crew concerning height and speed and heading, they would apply the ballistics of the particular type of sensor to project where the unit had (probably) landed. This information would then be given to the guys who programmed those computers which were monitoring the sensor's signals.

The sensors would normally be dropped in a string of six. Knowing where each one was and the distance between them allowed those monitoring the signals to note the time each one was triggered. The intelligence people would try to analyze the signal received to determine what had triggered the unit. Calculating how fast whatever had passed was going they would then guess when it would reach wherever they thought it might be going.

The seismic sensors transmitted vibrations. The audio sensors transmitted sounds; trucks passing, troops passing and even people talking. We had interpreters to make out what they were saying.

One of those interpreters, so the story goes, was listening to the input from an audio sensor when he burst out laughing. It broke the silence and intensity of others who were listening to other sensors. They asked what was the joke?

These were times when the official word was that we had no personnel in Laos. We did, in fact, have road watch teams there. These teams would radio back what intelligence they could gather. The Viet Cong knew, they were aware these teams were there – somewhere.

"Charlie," as the Viet Cong was commonly called, had discovered one of our audio sensors hanging high in a tree. These (at least two) guys that spied it thought it might be supplies we were dropping to a road watch team. I would guess their supply chain didn't include catered dining. From their conversation they thought there might be something to eat in that can up in the tree.

The fella monitoring could tell, by the volume increase and other sounds, that one of the guys was climbing the tree. As he got nearer there was the sudden sound of branches breaking. He heard the fella holler. The guy evidently fell out of the tree. A little bit of slap-stick humor in the middle of a war.

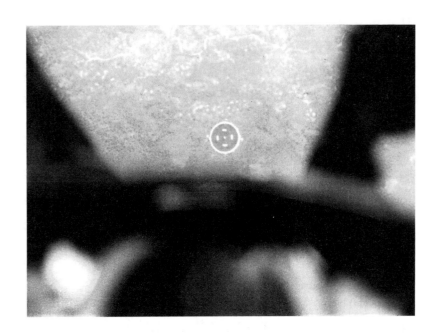

View through the windscreen during a

dive-bombing attack on the

Ho Chi Min trail

Placing Sensors

There's a rule in aerial warfare that a person disregards at their own peril: never fly straight and level for any period of time. Gunners, sighting at you from the ground, like nothing better than to be able to predict where you're going to be.

In the air the rule is to always "check your six." Directions in the aircraft are likened to the face of a clock: Twelve o'clock is straight ahead, six o'clock is your tail and so forth. "Check your six" means to always be aware if someone is coming up behind you. A good many guys got shot down by an aircraft they didn't even know was there.

Our Igloo White mission, placing a string of sensors along a road, path, etc., required straight and level flight for an extended period. The altitude of delivery was such that we would be within the lethal range of enemy guns and present a pretty tempting target. One of the ways we tried to counter this threat was to come in low and as fast as the sensor delivery parameters allowed. We tried to arrive as unexpectedly as we could.

Unfortunately one of the rules that we, "the good guys," had to comply with was that we couldn't drop any ordinance on Laos without a forward air controller (FAC) examining the area and clearing the release.

The forward air controllers over Laos were usually flying little low-and-slow aircraft, Cessna 337s. Their job was to keep an eye on whatever was happening on the ground or what might have changed since their last flight. They carried white phosphorous rockets. They would fire a rocket to mark a target or, in our case, mark the spot where we were to drop the first sensor.

A white phosphorous rocket, when it detonates upon contact with the ground, gives off a large cloud of white smoke, very easily seen from the air. Once they fired a rocket, Charlie pretty well guessed there was a whole world of hurt coming his way. He might have been trying to hide, not fire at the FAC and give away his position. Once the rocket was fired he might think he had nothing to lose. He'd start shooting. They were a pretty gutsy bunch, those forward air controllers.

The Wing Intelligence section had all sorts of information on the threat we, the air crews, would be facing over hostile territory. Most of the antiaircraft fire we were facing up and down the Ho Chi Minh trail was from 37mm antiaircraft guns.

We carried Electronic Counter Measure equipment in our aircraft which pretty well cancelled out their gun laying radar. Their fire was mostly an eyeball operation hence the no straight and level flight rule.

A 37mm antiaircraft gun had an optimum range – and I'm reaching back a ways here so bear with me – from about a thousand feet to 3,700 feet. At ranges greater than 3,700 feet the shell's trajectory was pretty well dissipated. Closer than 1,000 feet, well, if any of you are duck hunters, you know that when the duck flies right across in front of your blind you hardly have a chance to raise your gun.

We, delivering those sensors, were between those two range figures. That's why we tried to get in and out as fast and as unexpectedly as we could.

We had one guy, no matter how he did the job, always seemed to come back with holes in the aircraft. "Old magnet butt," we used to call him. When I rotated back to the 'states the guy was still flying. I don't know if he survived the war or not.

My back seater and I developed another tactic that may have helped our survival. As I said, the lethal range of those guns was 1,000 to 3,700 feet. When dropping bombs the delivery was usually from 7,000 feet or so.

We didn't use that "pull up and over the top" maneuver that you see in all the movies. Some guys did. My thought was that by doing that, a person was just giving the guy on the ground that much more time to adjust his sights, charge a round into the chamber and get a comfortable sight picture. Denny and I used to quickly roll the aircraft about 135 degrees and pull the nose right down to the target.

I'd line up the sight picture and Denny would call off the altitudes. We'd release the bomb, as I remember, a couple thousand – maybe 2,500 feet – in the air. The next maneuver, followed by almost everybody, was to pull the nose up and climb out of that lethal range of fire.

Some fellas, particularly those on their first couple missions, would see those tracers coming up at them and, I guess, remember their home and family. They'd get wide eyed, punch the bomb delivery button and bury the stick in their stomach. Their idea was to get the nose up and get the heck out of there.

You've got to realize something here. When an airplane changes direction, especially when it does so suddenly, it doesn't follow a true, clean arc. It's like turning a speed boat on the water. If you turn suddenly, the bow comes around but the boat "mushes" sideways before it turns – and loses a lot of speed. The same thing happens with an airplane. That guy who buried the stick in his belly got the aircraft turned around but he had dissipated all his airspeed, his energy. He was pointed up but with very little energy left to get him out of the lethal gun range.

One of the secrets of flying is energy exchange. A pilot can trade altitude for airspeed or airspeed for altitude but yanking and banking just loses energy needlessly unless you're in a dogfight and you have to be especially careful wasting it there. There's a toast, one pilot to another, that goes like this; "May you never run out of airspeed, altitude and ideas all at the same time." There's more philosophy to that than humor.

Back to the war. When Denny and I dropped a bomb, we didn't try to pull the nose up and get out of there. We'd keep descending, twisting and turning – "jinking" that's called. We'd level out at low altitude and get the heck away from the guns. Once out of range horizontally we'd climb back to altitude and get ready for the next attack. It seemed to work well. Denny and I came back.

You know, sometimes, when you've been working hard at a complex job and it's finished and it came out really good- maybe even better than expected- you experience a terrific feeling of elation? Multiply that by a factor of about ten and you can imagine the feeling when you've landed back to the "home 'drome" after having your butt shot at. Whooee! Sometimes you're on a high until an hour or more after the aircraft has landed.

Get 'em Out

I'm gonna give you a "war story" here. It has to do with those road watch teams in Laos I told you about.

There were airborne command posts. When entering the combat zone you'd check in with the airborne command post. They have your flight orders also. They'd send you to the forward air controller you were to work with and away you went.

Whenever someone was shot down or a ground team was in trouble the call would go out. The rest of the war would almost come to a stop while we tried to get the guys out.

Over Laos, if you were shot down and captured, the chances were excellent that you'd be killed. It wasn't that Charlie was mean or cruel but he was stretched pretty thin trying to get supplies down the Ho Chi Minh Trail. Prisoner of war compounds were back in North Viet Nam. Charlie had neither the time nor the facilities to guard and/or transport a prisoner. The expeditious thing to do was to shoot him.

We were told to try and let someone know, if we had to bail out or crash land in enemy territory, that we were still alive. The thought was that if Charlie was aware that someone knew you were on the ground and OK they'd be less likely to kill you. It would be harder to shrug and say you were killed in the crash. We all carried survival radios strapped to our parachutes, tuned to guard channel, a frequency everyone monitored. If you went down, call on guard channel to let someone know you're all right.

When something like that happened it was called a "Prairie Fire," as I remember. The airborne command post knew who all was in the area and what ordinance they were carrying. Getting the guy or guys out became job one.

On this day the command post sent us to a prairie fire emergency. We had cluster bombs as ordinance that day. I was leading in a flight of two.

Cluster bombs are a large bomb casing with several hundred small hand-grenade type bombs inside. Upon release, at a set altitude above the ground, the bomb casing opened. All those small bombs would spin and arm and scatter everywhere. When they hit the ground, they'd explode. There'd be fragments, shrapnel and they'd clear out a sizeable area.

When we contacted the FAC he was talking to us on our tactical frequency and to the guys on the ground on another frequency. This was keeping him pretty busy. We were working under an overcast layer at about 6,000 feet. We circled and waited.

When the FAC got a break he came up on our frequency to brief us on what was going on. Charlie had caught up to one of our road watch teams in Laos. In the ensuing fire fight two of the guys had managed to survive and get away. One of the guys was pretty badly wounded in his ankles. They had been able to contact this FAC who alerted the command post who sent us to the scene. At the moment they were hidden in the jungle with the bad guys all around searching and calling on them to surrender. Talking on the radio the team leader had to whisper to avoid revealing his position.

The FAC was having trouble locating where our guys were. He didn't want to send us in with cluster bombs until he knew and could avoid where our guys were hidden. We circled some more.

There's a minimum quantity of fuel we must have to be able to return to our base in Thailand with the required reserve. When any aircraft in the flight gets down to that fuel level they declare "Bingo Fuel." That means it's time to go home.

We circled for maybe ten more minutes. The FAC was evidently talking with the guys on the ground. He would fire a rocket every now and then. The white smoke would rise and then slowly dissipate. He was checking with our guys to see if either of them could see his last rocket.

We continued to circle below that low ceiling. After a few minutes more my wingman called "Bingo Fuel."

The overworked FAC came on the air and snapped, "Listen, you guys. Those are Americans down there. If we don't do somethin', they ain't gonna make it."

I rogered his transmission and said "Gimme a minute."

"Denny, what's the nearest friendly base?"

Quick as a flash Denny came back, "Phan Rang in South Viet Nam, its XX minutes." Aah, that Denny. He was sharp as a razor and right on top of the problem. He was probably ahead of me with that thinking."

"What's our new bingo fuel using Phan Rang?"

"XXX pounds."

I called the FAC and told him we would stay with him. Then I called my wingman giving him the new recovery base and the new bingo fuel amount. He acknowledged and we continued to circle.

The FAC came up on frequency to review what he had found out with us. He identified landmarks below and told us where to drop and where to avoid. He had two small helicopters standing by clear of the combat area. They would swoop in and pick up our guys as soon as we had driven Charlie from the recovery area.

Over the next twenty or thirty minutes my wingman and I each made two passes. We delivered ordinance, cluster bombs, both times. It looked like it was working. We had evidently chopped up a bunch of the bad guys and the rest were trying to find a safe place to hide.

My wingman called. "Bingo fuel." The fight was still going on. I told him he could break off and head for Phan Rang. He rogerd my call, pulled up and left. Denny and I stayed.

"You realize we have less fuel than he had." It was Denny. Not questioning the decision, just a stating a fact.

"How much fuel to get to Phan Rang, Denny?"

"XXX pounds"

"Lemme know when we're down to that much."

We circled some more.

The FAC called in the helicopters. They were what they called "Slicks," not big birds. There were two of them. one for each of the two guys on the ground.

I keyed my microphone. "FAC, we can make one more pass. All I've got left is a pod of rockets but we'll throw the wing tanks at 'em if you think that'll help. If we don't get outta here now we'll be down there with them."

"Give 'em the rockets, just left of your last pass but keep the wing tanks. You may need them.

Denny and I saddling up

Thanks for your help."

"Our pleasure. So long and good luck."

We made it to Phan Rang with about two minutes of fuel to spare. They had a set up called "hot-pit refueling." refueling an aircraft with the engines running. That last two minutes of fuel we had allowed us to taxi to the fuel pit and hook up. The flight back to Ubon was uneventful.

Did I mention what a heck of a good man my back seater, Denny Lipp, was? Even if I did it's worth mentioning again. There's nothing that bonds guys together like the fire of a life-or-death fight.

We found out later that the helicopters had been able to pick up both guys. Unfortunately there's still a casualty in this story. The guy that was wounded in the ankles didn't make it. Evidently the two helicopters only had external seats for the guys they picked up. The wounded fella, evidently in great pain hadn't secured himself to the seat and fell from the helicopter. The helicopter was at an altitude of 6,000 feet at the time. .

The date this happened was November 15, 1968, my 39th birthday.

To go or Not to go

Getting shot at every day gets a person thinking about what's important in life. It can lead to nights lying alone on your bunk and staring into the darkness.

For many of the younger troops it was all a great adventure. There would be some pretty wild parties in the club. To younger guys their belief seems to be that they're eternal. There may be a couple reasons for that. One is that they're still young and, the second, that they're not in the front seat where they see all that flak coming up at them. I don't know maybe there are more reasons.

On Sundays a person would have trouble finding a seat in a pew at any of the church services, Catholic, Protestant, maybe even the atheists if they held a service. Suddenly it was "nearer, my God, to thee" - and probably with good reason. For me, and I attended some of those services, I guess I'm an agnostic. I think there's a God but I don't think anyone down here knows much about Him or Her or It as the case might be. If I was God I think I'd knock a few heads and straighten us out down here on earth.

The two Chaplains, one was Catholic and the other, I believe, was Baptist, were really good guys. They were very often in the officer's club. They didn't drink that much but I think it was a good place for them to be, on "standby" you might say.

We were involved in a major aerial strike against North Viet Nam one day. We and aircraft from another base were all going north together on a big strike. We were trying to get everybody off the ground as close together as we could.

Maintenance crews and equipment technical representatives were standing by at the launch end of the runway. If anyone had any problems the people were right there to try to repair it.

Each of the various maintenance departments and technical representatives wore jackets with their systems printed in large letters on their backs. The Catholic Priest was out there too. On his jacket it read "Vatican Tech. Rep." The Baptist Preacher might have been out there too, I don't know.

Sometimes we'd sit around the club with those Chaplains, have a drink, just soda pop a lot of the time, and have some pretty serious discussions. We'd talk about life and death and why people were trying to kill each other and anything and everything in between. These Chaplains didn't revert rolling their eyes and ceremonial whoop-dee-doo. They looked you in the eye and told it as straight as they could. They were good guys, those Chaplains.

Here and there among the fellas who were whooping and hollering there were others. They were a bit more sober – no pun intended. They might be sitting quietly by themselves with that "50 mission stare" away off into space. "Too many too close for too long."

The Club was open 24 hours a day. You could get a drink anytime. Maybe it had to do with relieving pressure.

There were others too. You'd see them gathered around a table and talking together. The conversations might be going something like this: "Do you know what target they sent me out for today? It was a foot bridge! It was a little bitty foot bridge across a creek away back in the bush. If we had blown it up, why, they'd of had it rebuilt before we got back home. That's foolish to risk a million dollar aircraft and crew for a target like that."

Others at the table would nod sagely in agreement, supporting the decision. Maybe they all sincerely felt that way. They agreed because in a minute they would speak telling a similar story. They'd be looking for support also. I don't want to judge these guys. History shows that, in many cases, the bureaucracy and the chain of command can make some pretty, well, inadvisable decisions. It calls to mind a verse from the "Charge of the Light Brigade" in the Crimean War of 1854.

"Forward, the Light Brigade!"
Was there a man dismay'd?
Not tho' the soldier knew
Someone had blunder'd:
Their's not to make reply,
Their's not to reason why,
Their's but to do and die:
Into the valley of Death
Rode the six hundred."

Afred Lord Tennyson

No one spoke aloud of "Bravery" or "Cowardice" or anything like that. Bravery is when you're the only one who knows you're scared. The guy who is truly "fearless," who is not afraid at all, needs psychological help. The guy who couldn't handle that fear – well – it's not for me to judge. We each have our breaking point.

I guess I was fatalistic – or maybe just not too smart. I always went where the order said go and tried my best to do what the order said do. I was usually scared too but don't tell anybody.

The shot-up tail assembly of a Forward Air
Controller's Cessna model 337 aircraft

Fighting in the Dark

Charlie moved most of his stuff, supplies and troops, down the Ho Chi Minh Trail at night. We had one squadron who specialized in night flying but the rest of us got in on some of it too. We didn't have our navigation lights on at night of course and Charlie didn't drive with headlights on either. We did have aircraft that carried flares which floated down under parachutes.

We tried to keep track of which trails Charlie was using most. We did this through the sensors we were planting and from the visual reconnaissance of the forward air controllers. Each FAC patrolled the same areas over and over and would notice any changes on the ground.

Once a trail had been selected we'd try to find a choke point. A choke point was somewhere that we could close off and they couldn't easily bypass.

Once we located such a point we'd attack it as late in the evening as we could. We'd drop 500 pound bombs to close it off. Then we'd drop delayed action 500 pound bombs. The delayed action bombs would "cook off" at irregular times preventing Charlie bringing in heavy equipment to re-open the trail. Lastly we'd "seed" the area with antipersonnel mines.

These antipersonnel mines were small grenade type devices. We'd spread hundreds of these from a low altitude so they'd be thick around our recent road cut. They were a bit bigger than a fist. When they'd land there would be a short delay before a number of small "doors" on each one would be released. Each door was spring loaded with a thin "fish-line" attached. This antipersonnel mine now had a spider web of fish lines strung out maybe thirty feet or so in all directions. Anything that moved one of those lines thereby disturbing the mine would cause it to detonate. It was lethal to the range of those lines. These were intended to keep Charlie from sending people in there to open the road.

As I said, we delivered these from very low altitude. Messing around at that low altitude one evening I ran our F-4 right through the top of a tall tree. The plane kept right on going and took us back to Ubon. They had to change both engines and straighten out a little tin when we got back though.

We tried to close off the selected choke point late in the evening in the hope that Charlie would not have time to get the word back up the trail and stop the trucks from starting down.

Next we'd wait a couple hours to give enemy traffic time to get down the trail and stopped at the choke point. If we had timed it right, the flare ship would overfly the area and release some flares. Under those flares we would be able to see if we'd "caught" anything.

If we had managed to trap some trucks, say, behind our road block we'd then hit the last truck to arrive thereby blocking any retreat route.

After that, with flares as needed, we'd chop up the rest of the convoy. Sometimes it worked and sometimes, well, you can't win them all.

Flying at night in a combat situation is pretty spooky. An attack pattern is set up with North as "twelve o'clock." As aircraft rolled in to attack or pulled off they are constantly announcing, "In from nine" or "Off to six." The idea is that everyone should know where everyone else is and where they're going.

Bumping together up there on a dark night can spoil your whole evening.

Another big problem is orientation. Human beings are accustomed to realizing their position by seeing (the horizon or something level), by muscular sense (when your seat is firmly in a chair you know which way is down) and by vestibular senses (the inner ear canal senses turns and such). In an airplane in the dark you can't see any horizon, your seat is usually firmly in the aircraft whatever its attitude and your inner ear canal gets sloshed around indiscriminately.

The aircraft flight instruments are what you have to rely on. If your attention is diverted you may not know what's happening. There's a strong possibility you may think you're going up when you're going down. One of the fellas who deployed to Viet Nam with me, I was a Squadron Flight Commander, flew into the ground like that one night.

I mentioned that my back seater, Denny Lipp, brushed the angel of death off our shoulders more than once. One of those times was at night. "Pull up!" he said. I did. Thank you.

There's a relationship that forms when you

share situations like that. It doesn't happen like the movies would have you believe. Those involved don't talk much about it. They'd probably be embarrassed if someone brought it up. As I said, it doesn't happen to everybody and there's no racial discrimination. You then know for sure who you can count on.

One of the reasons I made it home.

A good friend and the other half of

our crew, Dennis Lipp.

The Base is Under Attack

Ubon Royal Thai Air Force Base at Ubon, Thailand was somewhat removed from the fighting in Viet Nam. There were bad guys going up and down the Ho Chi Minh Trail in Laos but the border between Laos and Thailand was the Mekong River some sixty miles east. The bad guys were even further east than that.

Most of the folks in and around Ubon either liked Americans or put up with us. A lot of small shop owners welcomed our business. I'm not surprised if a lot of our Gis haven't bought polished bits of broken coke bottles thinking they were buying Emeralds. And, of course, there were the ubiquitous Seiko wrist watches. Whenever you saw someone with a Seiko wrist watch it was a dead giveaway they'd been to Southeast Asia

There had to have been a few folks whose sympathies were with Uncle Ho and the North Vietnamese but they weren't talkin' much.

The guys stationed "in country," in Viet Nam would have their troubles with attacks, usually at night and from rockets or mortars. We at Ubon weren't bothered with that. There were a couple times that I know of and I'm not sure about them. Let me tell you about it anyway.

We had Air Police that manned the gates and guarded the aircraft. We didn't have a sizeable base defense contingent but there was a plan. When needed clerks and cooks and other noncombat personnel would be mobilized. An alert would be sounded and they would proceed to assembly points. They would be issued rifles and stationed around the perimeter of the base.

One night, it must have been one or two in the morning, there was a banging on my bunkroom door. I'm pretty hard to wake up but this woke me. I was the flight commander and one of the troops was pounding on my door.

I stumbled out of bed and opened the door. "Yah. Wassup?"

"Listen!" the guy said. "Their mobilizing the defense force."

An Air Police pickup truck drove by. They were announcing on their loudspeaker, "Augmentees, report to your duty stations."

"Ya hear that? The base in under attack!"

I blinked hard a couple times trying to clear my head. "Has someone called us? What do they want us to do?" My immediate thought was they might want to fly out the aircraft.

"No! Nobody called."

"Well what are you waking me for?"

"Well," he replied, taken aback by my response, "I didn't want them to catch us in our undies."

We both had to laugh over that. In the meantime, thinking there might be something we could do, I picked up the barracks phone and called the squadron,

"Twenty-Fifth TAC Fighter. Sergeant Dooley."

Dooley was our personal equipment specialist who took care of parachutes, helmets, oxygen masks, things like that. He was also a guy who, if you approached him discretely, could probably get you a a pair of Ho Chi Minh's initialed pajamas.

"Dooley, this is Major Mukkala. What's goin' on down there?"

"We're under attack, sir."

"Is anybody down there? Is there any word what they want us to do?"

"No, there's nobody here but me, sir. I'm issuing the weapons."

"Issuing weapons? Who are you issuing weapons to?"

"I'm issuing them to the troops, sir. They ain't gonna catch us unarmed."

"Geezus, Pat! Don't send guys out in the dark with rifles. They're apt to be shootin' each other!"

"No sweat, sir. We ain't got no ammunition."

I may not remember the exact conversation verbatim, but that's the gist of it. Nobody shot anybody. In fact, there was no shooting at all.

It seems that a guard at the ammo dump, some half mile or so removed from the base, had called in that he was under attack. This triggered the whole base alerting system. You already know what happened from there.

The local Thai's were having an election. I suspect that a couple of the locals had dipped into a little too much "Mekong Moonshine" and were celebrating. Firecrackers set off in the dark near a remote guard station could have done the rest.

Another interesting story made the rounds

after our "attack." It seems the Wing Commander, the Deputy Commander and several staff people had been at a party at the Officer's Club. When the word came that the ammo dump was under attack they jumped into a staff car and headed for the ammo dump.

Off the base they were travelling down a Ubon street. Up ahead they saw a crowd of people, flares, shouting and they thought they had come upon the attackers.

None of them was armed. The disorganized crowd was moving down the street their way. Time to beat an orderly withdrawal. In attempting to turn around they managed to get the staff car stuck in a ditch.

Now Ubon did not have the sewage facilities of your average American town. In fact, Ubon's sewage facility was exactly what the commander and his staff were standing hip deep in trying to move the staff car.

The crowd arrived, all in a celebratory mood. They helped them get the car out of the ditch.

Now this particular story is classified a step or two above "TOP SECRET CRYPTO" so don't let the word get out.

A 2,000 year old stone

Buddha in Thailand

Shot Down!

For those of us flying over Laos and North Viet Nam there was always the possibility of being shot down or having to bail out over unfriendly territory. We all knew no one would be waiting for us with a brass band when we landed there. Escape and evasion had been a part of our training. Most of us had at least a half-formed plan as to how we would try to evade capture.

One of the flight crews flying out of Ubon, both the front and back seater, flew wearing a pair of those pole-climber spurs strapped on their lower legs. Their plan was to climb a tree and hide. I wasn't so sure that would work but it was their plan.

One guy had been shot down over Laos. He had bailed out and landed wide eyed and scared. The next thing that happened was a couple guys started shooting at him. This was Laos and, as I said, chances of capture rather than being shot were pretty slim. When they shot at him he decided they weren't interested in him surrendering.

Everyone flew with a small Air Force issue .38 revolver. Most of us also carried a little extra ammunition. This guy, after being shot at, decided if he was going down, he was going down swinging. He pulled out that little revolver, jumped up, shouting and firing as he charged these two guys with rifles. The two guys threw down their rifles and ran.

Another guy, a back seater in my flight, after hearing the previous guy's story, stocked up on ammunition enough to start a small war of his own. I was doubtful that that little .38 caliber revolver would hold up to that much firing but that was his plan. God help him if her ever bailed out and landed in a river. He'd sink like a stone.

Another survival item everyone carried was a small battery operated radio, a transceiver. It was pre-tuned to guard channel, 243.0 Mhz. Everyone in the air monitored that frequency in addition to whatever tactical frequency they might be using. If someone bailed out they tried to take out that radio and call "Mayday, Mayday, Mayday," (the international distress call). Tell someone who you are, where you were and that you needed help.

Whenever anyone was shot down the rest of the war assumed a secondary position. The airborne command post would assign the nearest Forward Air Controller as the on-scene-commander to coordinate rescue efforts. The command post knew who all was flying strikes in the area and what ordinance they had. Folks with suitable munitions – cluster bombs were always good – would be immediately diverted to assist the rescue.

The plan would usually be to "sanitize" the immediate area – drop enough explosives to all but make a desert of the area surrounding the downed man. Drive Charlie back before he had a chance to call in any of his own heavier weapons. Then came salvation.

Standing head and shoulders above all these efforts were the guys flying the rescue helicopters, the "Jolly Green Giants." After the rest of us had sanitized the recovery area as best we could, these guys would come in to pick up the downed man.

They would drop a line with a thing called a jungle-penetrator, a steel rod that had folding arms that could be extended. The idea was for the guy to extend these arms, straddle the rod and while sitting on the extended arms the chopper crew would winch him up – while getting the h—l out of there of course.

In those situations where the man on the ground was disabled or for some reason couldn't get on the jungle penetrator, one of the chopper crewman would go down and help him. To the rest of us, those guys were a pretty tall-walkin' bunch.

Two of these Jolly Greens landed at Ubon one evening. We met them with a crew van. Their feet never touched the ground. We took them directly to the Officer's club. They got anything they wanted to eat or drink and we wouldn't let them pay for a thing.

The Club officer, upon realizing that some of these helicopter crewmen were enlisted men, thought that maybe they shouldn't be in the Officer's Club. We "reasoned" with him a little, a pretty fair sized bunch of us. Actually, once he realized the situation, he was with us all the way.

He was a good ole boy.

Who Gets a Medal?

Medals are the military equivalent of bonuses or stock options. Some simply say that you served in a particular area. Others say you did a darned good job while there. Still others are in recognition of something you did that was really outstanding. I think they're an excellent means of recognition and reward. Like everything else in life they sometimes miss someone or are "arranged" through political situations. All in all, they're a good thing.

I was at the edge of that business for a while. I wrote up and sent in recommendations. Many people were recommended, recognized. and received awards. My congratulations to them. Unfortunately there were also many who were deserving but, for one reason or another, never received the recognition.

I did what I could and tried not to overlook anyone.

You have never lived
till you almost died.
And for those who fight for it,
life and freedom has a flavor
the protected will never know.

The Frustrations of War

I may be getting off the reservation but I'm the one writing this book. This is something I want to say. Wars are the most wasteful and brutalizing of human endeavor anywhere.

Ho Chi Minh was probably the most effective leader in Southeast Asia. I don't know what his politics were and I don't think anyone else was really sure either. Somebody points a finger and yells "Communist!" and we fight against him. The guys we were defending seemed to be opportunists motivated by self-interest.

I was in the military. My response was, "Yes, Sir!" Left face, forward march. Without that discipline our nation would have anarchy.

Some of the guys had "T" shirts with the inscription, "Kill 'em all. Let God sort 'em out!"

"Raven" FACs were said to be CIA. We were told, if they called us, to go where they said go and do what they said do, no questions.

Two of us answered their call one day. We

dropped cluster bombs on a dense jungle. There was nothing there we could see. A week or two later I was told that a body count found over 400 bodies.

Do you remember Lt. Calley? The guy who had his troops shoot up a bunch of people in a ditch? He wasn't the sharpest tool in the shed but I can understand how he might have lost it. The paramount rule is, "the last man standing is the winner."Am I saying good things about Lt. Calley? Or bad things about me? I don't know.

There was a take-off on a Christian prayer: "Yea though I walk through the valley of the shadow of death I will fear no evil – 'cause I'm the meanest SOB in the valley."

Guys who've "been there, done that," have memories that haunt them the rest of their lives. Some may bring that brutality back home with them. Evidence of the problem is in the high number of suicides among current Iraqi veterans.

Iraq! Afghanistan! Pakistan! Iran! Palestine! Israel! Georgia! Where else? There's gotta be a better way.

Back Home Again

Denny and I flew our last mission, packed our bags and headed home. We cycled through Saigon on the way home. It was the end of the month.

Some staff troops from Air Transport Command were flying the airplane I came out on. There was "combat pay" or a tax deduction or something a person got each month they were in Viet Nam. These staff people would schedule themselves into Saigon on the last day of the month, spend the night and depart the first of the next month. That way they qualified for two months. It was a practical thing to do. These crews weren't always as well versed in handling and caring for the troops they carried home. The guys didn't seem to care. They were going home.

The night we spent at the base in Saigon there was a mortar attack. The barracks was pretty well protected with sand bags. Some of the once-every-other-month transport crewmembers were outside, in the dark. They had tape recorders and were running around holding up a microphone to record the sounds of the attack. You make up your own mind about that.

Back stateside I had been assigned to the 305th B-58 Bomb Wing at Bunker Hill Air Force Base (later to become Grissom Air Force Base) in Indiana. This was in 1969 and President Nixon was cutting the budget. The B-58s were being retired, scrapped, down in Tucson, Arizona. Reserve officers were being discharged. I was a reserve officer.

August of 1970 would mark twenty years in the Air Force for me, the minimum time for retirement. I flew the B-58 for a while longer, 'til they retired, then I became a sort of fifth wheel on the wagon.

I was assigned as Chief, Base Operations and Training but my heart wasn't in it. I was eligible for promotion to Lieutenant Colonel but, with retirement coming up, I guess they figured it would be a promotion slot wasted. Maybe there were other reasons.

In May of 1960 the opportunity arose to ferry a C-47 from McClellan Air Force Base near Sacramento, California, across the Pacific Ocean to Jakarta, Indonesia. I volunteered.

C-47 "Skytrain
The "Gooney Bird"

The Wide Pacific

The flight to California was by commercial air. When they assembled a crew at McClellan I was assigned as Aircraft Commander since I had the most C-47 flying experience.

My co-pilot was a lieutenant colonel I had known in the B-58s as was the navigator, a major. The radio operator was a sergeant I remembered form my B-36 maintenance days back at Carswell in Fort Worth, Texas. Our crew chief I had never met before but he turned out to be one of the best of the bunch.

Comparing notes we found that we were all about to be discharged – "The Retirement Express." we dubbed our aircraft.

This C-47 had been fitted out with fuselage tanks to carry enough fuel for the long overwater flight. There were to be three C-47s going to Indonesia. We weren't a formation. Each aircraft would go on its own.

The distance from McClellan to Hawaii is just over 2,400 miles. The old "Gooney Bird" traveled about 150 miles per hour give or take but there would probably be headwinds. We were going to be in the air awhile.

I had been taking night school and correspondence courses since 1954. I was hoping to get a degree before going out into the cold cruel civilian world. Ball State University at Muncie, Indiana, had been offering courses at Grissom Air Force Base and I had enrolled.

After takeoff from McClellan and getting established on course out over the ocean, I asked the copilot to keep an eye on the flying. I went to the back of the airplane and sat down among the auxiliary fuel tanks. I spent a good bit of the flight studying and writing the reports for those courses I was taking.

The auto pilot was old and a bit weary but, with a little adjustment now and then, it held course and altitude.

The navigator kept track of our position, "shot the sun" with his sextant and plotted our positions. The radio operator reported the positions as the navigator provided them. I read my books.

The copilot and I spelled each other now and then for a nap or just a break. Sometimes we just sat in the cockpit and swapped war stories, you know, as pilots are prone to do.

The flight to Hawaii took sixteen and one half hours. We arrived in Honolulu in the dark.

We had to spend three or four days in Hawaii as there was a weather system between Hawaii and Midway Island. If you're going to be stuck somewhere for a few days, Honolulu is the place to be. We rented a car and went touring.

Finally the weather system appeared to be breaking up. All three aircraft took a shot at flying on to Midway Island.

Once again we loaded up, took off and set a course for Midway Island some 1500 miles away. Things started out fine. About two thirds of the way there it began to look like the weather man had been a bit optimistic about that weather system dissipating. There were a whole lot of clouds and thunderstorms ahead.

One of the aircraft elected to divert north and try to get around the weather. A second guy elected to try to climb over it. I paralleled the thunderstorms southward a short ways, dipping down to see if we could go under them It looked pretty black and foreboding. I decided to reverse course. We didn't have fuel enough to make it back to Hawaii but there was a little island, French Frigate Shoals, about six hundred miles back with a Coast Guard contingent and a runway. That's about as big as that island at French Frigate Shoals was – a runway.

The navigator had been keeping track of our twists and turns – a technique called "air plot." There was no intercom on this airplane. I hollered back at him – the C-47 is not exactly a sound proof bird - for a heading for French Frigate

Shoals. He hollered back that he didn't have one. I hollered for "your best guess" figuring he'd give me a revised heading when he caught up with his calculations. He hollered back a heading and we turned to that.

On the radio I heard one of the other aircraft make a call "In the blind" - that they were uncertain of their position and were "surrounded by thunderstorms." I hollered to the radio operator to log that and any and all other calls he heard. Those guys were in a problem and we might be the only ones receiving them. If any of the aircraft turned up missing those calls might help locate their last known or "guestimated" position.

About then I heard another "mayday" call and turned to alert the radio operator. He was pale and wide eyed with his microphone to his lips. It was him making that call.

I asked the copilot to keep an eye on the flying. I got out of my seat and took the couple steps to the navigator's position. He was still pretty busy with his charts. The radio operator sat just across the narrow aisle from the navigator. He was staring up at me. I grinned at him and turned back to the navigator who looked up.

"How ya doin?"

He grinned and replied, "I'll have a better heading for you in just a minute."

"OK. Take your time." I walked on to the rear of the airplane to check on the crew chief. He was calm and relaxed and had everything under control.

A surreptitious glance back at the radio operator and he seemed to have relaxed a bit himself. I guess that calmer conversation between the navigator and myself soothed his fears. He seemed to have accepted that maybe everything was under control. I never mentioned that "mayday" call to him and he never mentioned it either. He was one scared radio operator there for little bit though.

The navigator came up with a refined heading and an estimated time to arrive at French Frigate Shoals.

The radio operator called our position and intentions to Hawaii. Hawaii alerted French Frigate Shoals that we were coming.

We arrived over French Frigate Shoals just as it was getting dark. The coastguardsmen had hurriedly set up empty drums along the edges of the runway with pans of gasoline on them. When they heard us approaching they lit the gasoline. That lighted runway looked beautiful! It was the only land within 500 miles. It was also the only dry place we could get to. The approach and landing was "just like downtown."

250' x 3,000' – the only land for 500 miles
French Frigate Shoals

Those guys at French Frigate Shoals seemed ever so happy to have anyone visiting them. They pulled out all the stops. There were about six of them, 500 miles from anywhere, manning a LORAN navigation radio and the station itself.

We had a delicious meal and, as I remember, their commander, Lieutenant JG, Hirsch, even pulled out a bottle of wine he had been hoarding.

We all toasted a safe arrival. After dinner they gave us a special showing of the movie: "True Grit" with John Wayne.

With their long range radio communication they offered to let us call home – no charge. We were all able to make telephone calls home. Because it was by radio, the calls had to be patched through a state-side station, and from there, "collect" to whoever we were calling.

I called my sister, Sandra, in Northern Michigan. Her husband, Don, answered the phone. He was told it was a collect call from Ben Mukkala from a place called French Frigate Shoals and would he accept the charges? He immediately thought I was in jail someplace and needed help. I've often wondered if that might not be a reflection of what he thought of his brother-in-law?

The troops refueled our plane by hand, "over the wing," from fuel drums. Those guys treated us like royalty.

The next day we took off and flew back to Hawaii. 458 miles. A routine 4 hour flight.

Two days later, after the weather system had dissipated, we took off again for Midway Island, 1,500 miles and six and one half hours away. We were getting pretty proficient at this take off and landing business by now.

One of the problems with landing at Midway Island are the Albatross'. These sea birds have been here forever and just assume they own the place. They're an independent creature that does what it wants when and where it wants without too much thought of the consequences.

They can take flight, much like we do with a run at it, and can soar out over the ocean for days – yes, literally for days – without ever landing. They evidently sleep while on the wing. Don't ask me how they do it.

On Midway they're apt to be strolling on the runway or maybe even nesting there. It's you who are attempting to land who is the inconsiderate

Albatross on Midway Island
Nickname: "Gooney Bird"

tourist. The C-47 received its affectionate nickname from the moniker folks attached to the Albatross: the "Gooney Bird."

The other two aircraft have been here and gone. We, other than the military contingent assigned, have Midway Island to ourselves – or as much as the "Gooney Birds" will allow. Walking down a path and encountering an Albatross, it would be you who had to detour around.

I have distinct memory of sitting alone on Midway beach in the moonlight with a cool drink in my hand. I looked at the sea and the sky and thought about God and me and the earth and the Gooney Birds and how was I so fortunate as to be here – things like that. It was a pleasant evening.

The next morning it was up and at it again. We'd been refueled and were ready to go thanks to our crew chief. The next leg of our journey would be from Midway to Wake Island some 1,200 miles away.

The weather was holding good and we were there in about seven hours.

When we landed we all went to a little bar on the station and had "a cool one." We were all pretty sweaty but seemed able to stand each other however I decided to go take a shower and put on a fresh flying suit.

When I got back an hour or so later the crew was still there. The copilot had gotten into some serious drinking. The rest of them were keeping him company but had slacked off considerably. The copilot had reached that stage where he was darn near incoherent. I don't tell you this to put down the guy (whom you don't and won't know anyway) but this next really happened. He looked up at me, bleary eyed and incoherent, and tried to say something. I don't know what it was he wanted to say but, as he looked at me, his eyes went in two directions. I don't mean together, I mean separately. I have never seen that happen before nor since.

The thought I had at the time was that, with the discharge from the Air Force coming up, maybe this was something more traumatic than he cared to admit? I guess it would have taken a professional "marble counter," a psychiatrist to understand it.

We managed to get the guy to bed. The rest of us got something to eat, and then hit the sack ourselves. There'd be another long flight tomorrow.

The next morning the copilot was in pain. The expression "death warmed over" comes to mind. I was concerned enough to ask if he didn't want to delay a day. He wanted to push on although he didn't eat any breakfast. We picked up flight lunches, checked out the airplane – the crew chief had everything in apple pie order – and took off. Our next port of call would be Guam, 1,500 miles away.

After take off we climbed to cruising altitude, leveled off on course and I engaged the auto pilot. The copilot seemed to have perked up a little but he still looked bad.

I asked him if he felt up to monitoring the aircraft if I went in back. He nodded his head, said he could handle it. I went back and got comfortable working on books and reports for my college courses.

I don't know how much later it was that I heard an angry shout from the navigator. I'm guessing it was less than an hour.

The navigator had been computing estimates of flying time to the next reporting point. He was dropping smoke flares to estimate wind speed and direction. He was calculating "speed line" sextant sightings for the sun. He was drawing intercept lines on his charts. The navigator keeps pretty busy on over-water flights of this length.

The navigator was seated at his tiny table, walled off from the cockpit just behind the pilot. There's a small clear plastic dome next to his position over the narrow walkway in the center of the aircraft. This clear dome is where he takes sightings with his sextant.

While he was poring over his charts, a ray of sunshine, shining through the sextant dome, moved slowly across his work. A short time later that ray of sunshine began moving slowly across his work again. He suddenly asked himself, why is that . . .

He got out of his seat and poked his head into the cockpit. The copilot was fast asleep and the aircraft was slowly flying in circles.

The navigator was ranting about calculating where we were and where we were going and what time we'd get there if the airplane was flying in circles.

This woke the copilot and got me back up to

the cockpit. We straightened the airplane out on course and re-engaged the autopilot. I stayed in the left seat in the cockpit. The copilot, having been severely chastised by the navigator, moped for, oh, maybe three or four minutes. Then he was once more fast asleep. Needless to say I stayed in the cockpit.

Eight and a half hours later we landed at Guam.

We spent a night at Guam – a very sober night, I might add and pressed on to Clark Air Base in the Phillipines, 1,600 miles and nine hours flying time later.

From Clark it was about 3,000 miles and eleven and a half hours to Jakarta, Indonesia.

The turnover thing was very casual. An Officer of the Indonesian Air Force met us, scrawled his signature across the receipt I had been given, and that was it.

We had left the 'states on the 8th of May, 1970, and turned the aircraft over to Indonesia on the 26th.

After a day or two we all flew back to Los Angeles on a commercial jet. It was strange, the way they computed our fare. It was a shorter "great circle" route from Jakarta to San Francisco than from Jakarta to Los Angeles, Because of that, so they said, the fare to San Francisco was a few dollars less than the fare to Los Angeles – even though the aircraft was landing at Los Angeles before going on to San Francisco? Strange.

I think it was the radio operator who was flying to San Francisco. The rest of us stopped at Los Angeles and each went our way from there.

When we arrived at Los Angeles and were parting, each to go his own way, I checked with our crew chief to see that he had everything under control. I knew immediately there was a problem.

He was one of those people who is hesitant to share his personal problems with others. I got him alone and pressed the question. It turned out he was short of money and didn't have enough to buy a plane ticket to get home.

The Air Force would pay his fare but he had to apply for the compensation. I was officially his commander for this trip. What we should have done, by the regulations, was contact the nearest military installation, submit the request for travel money, be paid, and proceed. This was a lot of screwing around.

I don't recall if it was credit cards or cash or a little of both. He and I got him a ticket home and a couple bucks to feed him on the way. He would apply for compensation at his home base. When he got paid, he would send me whatever amount it was that I had loaned him.

He did. End of story.

Into the Sunset

When I returned to Grissom I was still the Commander, Base Operations and Training. They had put a deputy in while I was gone. Technically I was still in charge but, since he would take over upon my discharge, just three months hence, I didn't rattle his cage.

The B-58s were phased out. They were being retired to Davis Monthan Air Force Base, the home for retired aircraft, at Tucson, Arizona. I wouldn't be sent to a base but I was being retired too.

Ball State University examined my college credits and service experience. They concluded that I had more than sufficient credits for a college degree. Unfortunately, with my moving around during my Air Force career I didn't have enough credits at any single university to qualify for a degree from any of them. Ball State agreed, however, that if I would attend there for two quarters, they would give me a certificate, a Bachelor of Science Degree. It took seventeen years but I am now a college graduate.

Let's see what the civilian world holds.

"Do what you love doing and you'll never work a day in your life."

Thanks.

Ben

Additional copies of this or any other of the
author's books may be purchased through:

Still Waters Publishing
257 Lakewood Lane
Marquette, MI 49855-9508

(906) 249 9831

www.benmukkala.com
bmukk@chartermi.net

at the following prices:

"Thoughts Along the Way" $ 15.95
"Life is Not a Destination" $ 14.95
"Touring Guide; Big Bay & Huron Mountains $ 9.95
"Come On Along" $14.95
"Copper, Timber, Iron and Heart" $15.95
"Gift of Wings" $15.95

Please add for shipping and handling $ 5.00

Enjoy!

Ben Mukkala

Author

Ben Mukkala is a native of Marquette, Michigan where he graduated from Gravaraet High School and Ball State University in Indiana. He enlisted as a private in the U. S. Air Force during the Korean War, rose through the ranks and served a tour of duty in Southeast Asia flying F-4 "Phantom" jet fighter-bombers in the Viet Nam conflict. Ben retired in 1970 with the rank of Major.

He is the father of three daughters and one son and stepfather to two sons and four daughters and a whole bunch of grandchildren. He currently lives with his wife, Dorothy, on the shore of Lake Superior in Marquette, Michigan.